A History of Brussels Beer in 50 Objects

A History of Brussels Beer in 50 Objects

First Published July 2022

Copyright © 2022 Eoghan Walsh

ISBN 979-8-8129037-2-5

Image credits:

#5 (p.29) © Coudenberg Palace, collection Brussels Capital Region, photo M. Vanhulst; #7 (p.37) © Musées de la Ville de Bruxelles – Maison du Roi; #10, #12 (p.49, p.57) © Collectie Museum van de Belgische Brouwers; #24 (p.105) Espace Nord; #34 (p.145) Musée De La Bière Schaerbeekois; #35, #39 (p.149, p.165) Jean Goovaerts/Brasserie de la Senne; #46 (p.193) Brasserie En Stoemelings; #47 (p.197) Julien Kremer/Nanobrasserie L'Ermitage; #49 (p.205) Amaury Dastarac/Brasserie de la Mule

Cover illustration and design: Selkies

Book design: Ruairí Talbot

All rights reserved. No part of this book may be reproduced in any form or by any electronic or mechanical means, including information storage and retrieval systems, without permission in writing from the publisher, except by reviewers, who may quote brief passages in a review.

For more information, contact: eoghan@beercity.brussels

www.beercity.brussels

A History of Brussels Beer in 50 Objects

Eoghan Walsh

Praise for
"A History of Brussels Beer in 50 Objects"

"One of the most consistently fascinating projects in beer writing. Transports you through time and brings a complex beer culture to life."

Jessica Boak and Ray Bailey, authors of *20th Century Pub*

"This original beer book leads us to the many bigger and smaller crossroads towards the making of Brussels as a beer capital."

Sven Gatz, Brussels politician and Belgian beer lover

"Eoghan Walsh has taken a flea market and turned it into a meditation on history, culture, and place. Piece by piece, these fifty objects create the colourful mosaic of a city with beer running through her veins."

Jeff Alworth, author of *The Beer Bible*

"A brilliant examination of Brussels beer culture, and essential reading for beer enthusiasts and Belgophiles alike."

Breandán Kearney, award-winning author and founder of *Belgian Smaak*

For Lore, Noa, and Zoey

Thanks for sacrificing your Saturday mornings

Table of Contents

Introduction

2 million BCE-1300s
1. Brasserie Cantillon Coolship — 13
2. Zenne River Water — 17
3. Head of Barley — 21
4. Bruxella 1238 — 25
5. Cruche — 29

1565-1700s
6. Pieter Bruegel the Elder's *The Harvesters* — *33*
7. *In Het Carosseken inn sign* — 37
8. Statue of Karel van Lotharingen — 41
9. Brewers' Oath — 45
10. Statue of St. Arnoldus — 49
11. Entrance to Het Heideken — 53
12. Bierkruk — 57
13. Schaarbeekse Kriek — 61

1800-1895
14. Lambikstoemper — 65
15. Bottletop, marchand de bières — 69
16. Fromage de Bruxelles — 73
17. Zagemanneke — 77
18. Koekelberg Bock Beer — 81
19. De La Vergne Compressor — 85
20. Hotel Continental Stein — 89
21. *Les Mémoires de Jef Lambic* — 93
22. Tire-Bouchon — 97
23. Le Petit Journal du Brasseur, № 1 — 101

1910-1994
24. *Le Mariage de Mlle Beulemans* — 105

25. Dog Ale Matchbox 109
26. Plan for Brasserie Léopold 113
27. Rue Brederode 117
28. Gueuze Belle-Vue 121
29. Vandenheuvel New Year's Card 125
30. «Curiosités et Anecdotes: La Gueuze» 129
31. Three Stars Pils Playing Cards 133
32. '81-'82 Anderlecht Team Photo 137
33. Jaar Van Het Bier Tankard 141
34. Musée De La Bière Schaerbeekois Beer Mats 145

2002-2010
35. Sketches for a Zinnebir Label 149
36. Moeder Lambic Serviette 153
37. *Around Brussels in 80 Beers* 157
38. Zwanze 2009 161
39. Brussels Calling 165

2013-2021
40. Brussels Beer Project Alpha 169
41. Malt Attacks Growler 173
42. Vini Birre Ribelli Glass 177
43. Rue du Miroir 1 181
44. Pistolet Original Belgian Hot Dog 185
45. SKOL Bottletop 189
46. Papy Van De Pils Label 193
47. L'Ermitage Summer Krump 197
48. Support Local Breweries T-shirt 201
49. Brasserie de la Mule Hefe Weisse 205
50. Brussels Beer Project's Coolship 209

Introduction

How do you weave together 12 centuries of cultural, economic, geographic, demographic, culinary, and industrial history into a digestible narrative?

That was the question I posed myself in a moment of creative inertia in early 2021. We were almost one year into the pandemic, my writing inspiration was running low, and mentally I was beginning to fray a little at the edges. If my work on Brussels Beer City was going to continue, I needed a writing project.

In the year leading up to spring 2020, I had left my job - temporarily - in an attempt to gauge whether I had the mentality and the character to become a full-time freelance writer. It turned out I did not, or at least I was not prepared to find out during a deadly global virus outbreak. So I returned to steady employment and continued to work on Brussels Beer City in my free time. But it was a slog, and my writing suffered. I can see that now, looking back at the hodgepodge of subjects and formats - podcasts, listices, interviews - I published then. And with the pandemic causing upheaval in my personal life, it was increasingly hard to make room in my calendar for writing without it complicating the regularly-scheduled programming of life with two small children.

So, as I said, I needed a project. An idea for a series of articles that would force me to work to a regular publishing rhythm, that could be planned in advance, which once set in motion would take on a momentum of its own and not require me to expend creative energy on coming up with new writing topics.

It was always going to focus on Brussels beer history. I briefly considered following the lead of Fernand Braudel and his deep-time *Annales* colleagues, committing to a decades-long, rigorously academic treatise on the longue durée of Brussels' social, economic, and political history. But then I remembered I'm an amateur historian, pressed for time and resources, and unable to spend hours every day locked away in Brussels' Koninklijke Bibliotheek.

I was better taking inspiration from a less baroque source. Something like Dr Neil MacGregor's A History Of The World In 100 Objects, a book and cross-platform project launched in 2010 by the BBC and the British Museum. From stone axes to solar powered lamps, they explained human history through artefacts from the museum's collection. The project received criticism for its perceived lack of self-reflection on the origin of several objects, and their links to Britain's colonial past, but as a way of briskly explaining history in a meaningful and engaging way, it succeeded.

It is a template that has since been replicated to cover histories as varied as the middle ages, intellectual property, gardening, and the Apollo moon missions. So why would it not work for Brussels' illustrious beer history, albeit reducing the size of the series from 100 to 50 objects. This would allow me to parcel out this story in manageable weekly entries. And, because creativity thrives under constraints, I added one more requirement: each article of this prospective new series was to be 500 words long. No more, no less; 500 exactly.

And so, "A History Of Brussels In 50 Objects" was born, with the first entry - Brasserie Cantillon's coolship - published on Friday, July 16, 2021. From then until July 2022 - coincidentally the fifth birthday of the publication of my first ever post as Brussels Beer City - a short article would appear charting some aspect of Brussels beer history. Each object told a different aspect of Brussels' interconnected beer and urban histories. Early objects covered the city's early medieval founding on the banks of the marshy Zenne river as a pastoral community, and this village's gradual emergence as an economic, trade, political and ecclesiastical centre under Charles V during the early Renaissance. Later, the chosen objects charted Brussels' tumultuous centuries of war and occupation by successive waves of invading French and German armies, before its rise, fall, and rise again as an independent Belgium's industrial, economic, and brewing powerhouse. The higher the object's number, the more contemporary the history, and the closer we get to Brussels' early 21st century unexpected beer and brewing revival.

Now, it's important at the outset to say that, as you'll see, I'm interpreting the idea of an "object" pretty liberally. There will be the types of objects you might expect - brewing equipment for example, or old beer bottles and drinking vessels. But there are also books, plays, blueprints, film, and agricultural produce. Brewing has left many marks on the urban fabric of the city, and it would be remiss of me not to include some of them, which explains the inclusion of industrial equipment, buildings, and in one particular case, a whole street. The only criterion i set for an object's inclusion was that it had to say something about Brussels' beer traditions - making it, selling it, drinking it, celebrating it.

For narrative coherence, objects occupy vaguely-defined categories. *Brewery Life* tells the changing story of how beer was made, and *Business Life* the influences behind these decisions. *Pub Life* explores Brussels' café culture. *City Life* takes in the city's wider social, geographic, economic and political contexts. And *Food Life* represents the influence of agriculture and culinary trends, and how that relationship has changed over the centuries.

"A History of Brussels Beer in 50 Objects" is *a* history, not the history. The objects I've selected bend towards my subjective historical interests, and necessarily reflect some recency bias. The 19th, 20th and early 21st centuries will feature prominently because more artefacts from these eras exist, and because these were the most consequential periods of Brussels beer history. But there are other stories that don't get the attention they merit - the role of women, for one, and some of the more obscure brewing practices of the Middle Ages.

How do you weave together 12 centuries of cultural, economic, geographic, demographic, culinary, and industrial history into a digestible narrative?

Let's find out.

A History of Brussels Beer in 50 Objects

#1

Brasserie Cantillon Coolship
1937

- Brewery Life

It is not particularly old. Nor is it particularly impressive. But Brasserie Cantillon's coolship is living history. As the vessel where Lambic's alchemical brewing magic begins, it symbolises Brussels' unique centuries-long brewing tradition. And as Brussels' last active coolship, it binds that heritage to the city's modern beer scene.

Five metres squared, 30 centimetres deep, and housed in an attic room, the coolship was built out of salvaged spare brewery parts and installed when Cantillon started brewing in 1937. It is essential to the mythology of brewing Lambic, Brussels' indigenous beer style. Piping hot "wort", the sugary liquid produced by a lengthy brewing process, is pumped into the coolship, where it is left overnight for two reasons. First, the wort cools down gradually to 20°C thanks to the cool nighttime air. But it is a coolship's second function that helps make Lambic *Lambic*.

For fermentation, Lambic is inoculated not with yeast added by a brewer, but spontaneously by yeast and bacteria in the air and living on the walls and the wooden beams of the coolship room. This microflora makes its way into the wort as it rests overnight, before it is siphoned into barrels to begin fermentation. It was a view long-held by the region's brewers that Lambic brewing was only possible here because of the Zenne valley's unique microbiome.

Cantillon is the great survivor; it was the only one of its 20th century Brussels contemporaries that survived the obliteration of traditional Lambic brewing by the advent of industrialisation. It did so by becoming living history, surviving the 1970s and 1980s by becoming a working museum. Under Jean-Pierre Van Roy's stewardship Cantillon emerged in the 1990s and 2000s to ride the cresting wave of interest in Belgian beer to financial stability. Then came an explosion of interest in the complex and tart flavours of their beers, as a global subculture of Lambic aficionados emerged to journey to Cantillon's Anderlecht home.

Buoyed by this popularity, Jean-Pierre's son Jean began pushing beyond Lambic's traditions to experiment with new fruit blends and exploring new flavours discovered through his connections with French and Italian viticulture. When a slew of breweries opened in the 2010s, Van Roy became a supportive elder statesman to a new generation of uncertain brewers seeking advice, access to raw materials, and a sense of community. Yvan De Baets of Brasserie de la Senne clocked in some time at Cantillon as did Joel Galy before opening his Brasserie de la Mule. Cantillon's influence on the contemporary beer scene is inescapable - in its adherence to a certain ascetic "way of doing things", in the emphasis on quality raw materials, in the respect for - and willingness to occasionally transgress - tradition.

The beers aren't to everyone's tastes. And Cantillon has received criticism for antediluvian beer labels and ill-considered entertainment choices. But it remains a foundational part of Brussels' beer community. The brewery, and its coolship, represents the twin forces of continuity and adaptability that have been a hallmark of Brussels beer through the centuries.

A History of Brussels Beer in 50 Objects

#2

Zenne River Water

2 million BCE (sample collected July 2021)

- City Life

Brussels was born where, on a narrowing bend of the Senne river, the valiant Saint Gorik of Cambrai slayed a troublesome dragon.

Brussels was born where, on a narrowing bend of the Senne river, a Duke of Lower Lotharingia built a fortified camp.

Brussels was born where, on a narrowing bend in the Senne river, a loosely-connected network of villages on the riverbank coalesced into an urban settlement.

Two of these are myth and one is as close to a factual retelling of the founding of Brussels' first millennium origins as you'll get. But they share a common character: the Zenne. Brussels exists because of the Zenne. When the city makes one of its first textual appearances in 966 as *Broucsella*, it's watery origins are already clear - the name is a combination of *brouc* (brook or marsh) and *sele* (habitation). And it was on the steep banks of the Zenne that Brussels gradually emerged in the 11th and 12th centuries as an economic, political, and ecclesiastical centre. The river was central to the lives of these early inhabitants. It slaked their thirst, powered their mills, connected traders in Antwerp and the Rhine, irrigated their crops, and sustained their fisheries.

It also lubricated their breweries. Right from its founding, Brussels' residents tinkered with the Zenne, digging channels and creating new man-made islands. The *Grand Île* was one of these, engineered in the 11th century and home to a church honouring the mythical dragonslayer. It was here that the densest congregation of Brussels breweries emerged, remaining a brewing centre even as the Zenne's influence on Brussels' form and function declined. These were household breweries, or breweries in outhouses, cantilevered over the river and brewing for the neighbouring streets in the most populous district in Brussels. The earliest brewers harvested the Zenne to make beer, their successors extracting water to clean their equipment.

When this early modern artisanal occupation morphed into a semi-industrial business, the river was a useful outlet for brewery effluent. By the 1860s the brewers of the Grand Île (rechristened Place St Gery), alongside their neighbours the tanneries, paper factories, and textile producers, were complicit in the Zenne's irreversible corruption. In 1865 Brussels' city government voted to bury what was now a nauseating, miasmic, fetid stream. Above the river's brick sarcophagus came central Brussels' urbane Haussmannian boulevards, the building of which obliterated from the urban landscape the last remaining breweries of St Gery and centuries-long brewing heritage.

The Zenne still meanders furtively above-ground in Anderlecht, and its cultural memory and that of its tributaries survives. It's there in the names of districts like Etterbeek, Molenbeek, and Woluwe. Or in street names like Zennestraat or Rue du Pont, and in downtown Brussels' lumpy topography. Brussels' 21st century beer revival has brought breweries back to St Gery and surrounding streets, to brewi above the Zenne where predecessors would have worked next to it. Then there is Brasserie de la Senne, vanguard of this renaissance and named for the river that birthed its owners' beloved Brussels.

#3

Head of Barley

1000s (harvested July 2021)

- Farm Life

Dawn breaks early, again. A perky July sun escapes from behind eastern hills, infiltrating the slatted wooden bedroom walls. Rubbing away sleep, you grab your scythe, dusty yellow from yesterday's exertions. Outside, the muddy riverside path is baked hard from summer sun, the river quietly putrefying in the heat. It's a short, steep trudge up to the hilltop fields. The air is cold in your lungs, but it won't be long before you are drenched in a midday sweat. Cresting the ridge, you snake a glance over the quivering green tops of the high grass. Soon they'll be moving the relics from down on the big island. It'll be a while yet, though, looking at the state of those foundations. But sure, you have enough to be getting on with without worrying about the new chapel. After all, the barley won't harvest itself.

Barley fields have long vanished from the *Treurenberg*, Brussels' Hill of Tears, with the farmers who tended them. The humble chapel became a romanesque reliquary for St. Géry's remains before evolving into an imposing gothic cathedral. But traces of Brussels' agrarian origins remain. The dark soil of Dark Ages Brussels has, alongside telltale fecal evidence of animal husbandry and the chips and splinters of discarded earthenware, thrown up pre-12th century remnants of barley, wheat, oats, and rye.

Early Middle Age Brussels coalesced around sites like the Treurenberg and settlements along the river and at the *Oud Korenhuis* ("Old Grainstore"); at each, archeologists discovered evidence of crop growing. As these settlements merged and swelled, beyond the first city walls and out to a larger, pentagonal circumference of defensive fortifications, city planners continued to make room for fields of wheat, barley, and other grains.

The soil around Brussels was good soil for wheat and barley, a fertile seam of clay stretching north-east to south-west through Brabant. The fields fed people and their animals, and - presumably - to brew beers. A 17th century Brusselaar could choose from various-strength beers brewed to a standard recipe of six *sisters* (equivalent to 48.7 litres) of wheat, seven of barley, and four of oats. And it was wheat, and landrace varieties like the *Kleine Rosse van Brabant*, which came to dominate *Brabantse* brewing. Witbier in Hoegaarden. Peeterman in Leuven. Lambic in Brussels.

Urbanising Brussels outgrew its pentagonal boundary and eventually excised most of its farmland by the early 20th century. But beyond, in the Zenne valley's lumpy fields, farmers continued supplying Lambic brewers with their prized *Kleine Rosse* until more agronomically efficient crops supplanted it in the 1960s.

On Brussels' western edge, where the line between urban and rural muddles its way through the Pede river valley, are the last hardy vestiges of Brussels' pastoral backstory. There, next door to intruding electricity substations and redbrick bungalows, is a knot of cornfields, potato plantations, and several thoughtful small farms. And alongside the tuberous fields are patches of tall green and gold grasses twisting in the wind and waiting for the swish of their farmer's scythe.

#4

Bruxella 1238, Rue de la Bourse 8, 1000 Brussels

1238

- City Life

John - Duke of Brabant, The Victorious, first of his name - died on May 3, 1294 following a shemozzle with a minor nobleman during a wedding in northern France. John - or Jan, or Jan Primus - was born in Leuven and succeeded his father as Duke in 1267. In shifting his residence from his birthplace to Brussels' Coudenburg palace, Jan Primus tilted the axis of power away from the former and accelerated the latter's rise as Brabant's pre-eminent city. His burial in the graveyard of a cloister next to the Zenne river cemented Brussels' rise. What remains of his tomb now forms part of one of the city's less-heralded museums, Bruxella 1238.

So far, so minor medieval chronicle. But this particular Low Countries cove has an outsized reputation in Brussels brewing history. Because Jan Primus is better known as *Gambrinus* - King of Beer, patron of brewers, and mythical Germanic folk hero of beer drinkers. A popular figure in his own time, the 1911 *Encyclopædia Britannica* called Jan Primus "a perfect model of a feudal prince....brave, adventurous, excelling in every form of active exercise, fond of display, generous in temper."

He had a reputation for rousing military calls-to-arms while straddling beer casks, and "Hertog Jan" liked a drink, celebrating his triumph at the battle of Woeringen with a beer-drenched victory party. Brussels' 13th century brewers' guild honoured their political patron by installing an effigy of the duke in their meeting rooms. And Jan Primus is only, after all, a linguistic bastardisation or two from Gambrinus.

There are pretenders to his boozy throne. John "The Fearless", a Burgundian duke and Count of Flanders, claimed to have introduced hops to brewing, and in the 15th century established an Order of the Hops. Then there's Gambrinus' 16th century origins as mythical German king Gambrivius who learned brewing secrets from Egyptian deities. Or the 19th century story of a Cambrai glassblower who sold his soul to the devil to brew beer. But even the Germans accepted Gambrinus' Low Countries origins:

Gambrinus in leben werd ich genannt

Ein König in Flandern und Brabant

Aus Gersten hab ich malz gemacht

Und das bierbrauen daraus erdacht

"Gambrinus in life I am called

A king in Flanders and Brabant

I made malt from barley

And created beer brewing from it"

Jan Primus' bones have long disappeared from his riverside grave, the original monastery site having been destroyed in the paroxysms of iconoclastic fervour that gripped 16th century Brussels. The remains of the 13th century monastery, and Jan Primus' purported grave were eventually rediscovered during an archeological dig in 1988, alongside the foundations of Brussels 19th century Brussels' Stock exchange. As Bruxella 1238, they will be incorporated into the as-yet-unfinished Belgian Beer World visitor experience inside the stock exchange. Jan's bust still adorns a facade on Brussels' Grand Place, and continuing the veneration of their forebears in Brussels' medieval brewers guild, Belgium's Knights of the Brewer's Paddle toast the King of Beers each spring with an annual Feast of King Gambrinus.

Cruche
1300s

- Drinking Life

It doesn't look much, this jug. The rough earthenware surface is chipped, patches of oxidised orange blotting its grey sides. It is perforated in places, patched up in others. But it has largely kept its shape intact, bulging out at the middle before tapering at the spout. Or where the spout should be, because it has long since broken off. Which isn't much use for a jug (*cruche* in French). This jug, which might once have been filled with wine, oil, or beer, isn't aesthetically exceptional. It is special because it is roughly 700 years old, having spent most of its life buried in centuries of royal excrement at the bottom of an abandoned latrine in Brussels' Coudenberg palace.

The Coudenberg began as a defensive castle on a hill 40 metres above Brussels' medieval centre. It was part of Brussels' first ring of city walls built in the 14th century, but as the city expanded and those fortifications became redundant, the castle evolved into a ducal palace. By the 1500s, the palace was home to Charles

V, Holy Roman Emperor, King of Spain, Lord of the Netherlands, and patron of rapacious *conquistadors*. Charles would start his days in Brussels with a warm beer, and go from there. Breakfast of fowl at five in the morning, then mass. A 20-course noonday lunch of game from the nearby Warande hunting grounds, and heaps of oysters, eel pies and anchovies. More anchovies at eight, and a midnight supper.

Charles would wash it all down with lashings of chilled beer (or wine) - particularly beer from Mechelen, where he grew up - served from ceramic jugs into his four-handled mug. With this diet, it is no surprise gluttonous Charles regularly suffered debilitating attacks of gout. Such was his torment - and so incapable was Charles of tempering his appetite - that, bent double with gout and teary-eyed, he abdicated his throne in the Coudenberg's great hall on October 25, 1555. But before he left Brussels for monastic retirement in Spain, Charles placed one final order for beer from Mechelen to accompany him.

Thus ended Brussels' imperial phase, the Coudenberg's reputation thereafter declining until a fire destroyed it in 1731. Eventually a new, royal quarter was built on the ruins, centred on Place Royale atop the Kunstberg. Below this cobbled square are well-preserved parts of the palace's vaulted cellars and kitchens. But stone walls and crumbling mortar give little insight into the daily bustle of a court dedicated to sating the monarch's appetite. Better instead to resurface and walk downtown, to a dead-end alley café.

The upper walls of A La Bécasse are stacked with rows of ceramic jugs. Some are small, and some big enough to slake even a king's thirst. The pale blue glaze and smooth surfaces of these Lambic jugs are more polished than their 13th century ancestor. But they have inherited the same geometry, with slender bases, bulging midriffs, and tapering spouts instantly familiar to a gout-crippled emperor just waking up for his morning sup.

A History of Brussels Beer in 50 Objects

#6

Pieter Bruegel the Elder's *The Harvesters*

1565

- Farm Life

The Harvesters is class Bruegel.

The painting depicts an early autumn wheat harvest in the Pede valley. In the foreground a gaggle of farm labourers take a lunch break, eating pears, cheese and bread while in the background their colleagues continue working, scythes in hand. The background stretches away from the labourers into the valley, featuring nude monks frolicking in a lake and ships anchored in the distance.

One of the farm hands guzzles from a large ceramic *cruche*, and to their right through the wheat comes a colleague to replenish their beers, a jug in either hand. To judge by the frequency with which it appears in his paintings, Pieter Bruegel the Elder enjoyed a beer. Or, at least, he sympathised with his peasant subjects' appreciation of it. Beyond *The Harvesters*, beer is present alongside carousing farmers at *The Peasant Wedding*, in the grand guignol of *The Fight Between Carnival and Lent*, and in the festivities of *The Wedding Dance*.

Bruegel's life story is a bit of a puzzle for historians.

Born near Breda between 1525 and 1530, Bruegel moved to Brussels in 1563 and settled with his wife in a townhouse on the Hoogstraat. He painted *The Harvesters* there in 1565, and it was Brussels where he died in 1569; his body is buried in the nearby Kapellekerk.

Historians are usually sure about one thing, however. That Bruegel's peasants drank Lambic. Lambic is, as aficionados will take great joy in thoroughly explaining, one of the world's oldest beer styles, indigenous to the Zenne valley and made today largely in the same archaic way as in Bruegel's time.

Only, they weren't, and it isn't.

Bruegel did not paint Lambic-chugging peasants. He couldn't. Because Lambic did not exist in 16th century Brussels. At least, not according to Lambic historians like Raf Meert. I can already hear beer historians, clutching their copy of *Geuze & Kriek*, mewling about "absence of evidence is not evidence of absence". They will remonstrate about a tax clerk from the town of Halle called Remy le Mercier who, in 1559, wrote down rules for brewing beer with a grain bill featuring wheat and barley in similar ratios to those used for Lambic. Only, Monsieur le Mercier didn't call this beer Lambic. Bruegel was buried for two centuries before Lambic made its first written appearance, in the papers of a 1794 payment dispute in Brussels between a brewer's widow and a local bar owner about "*quattre tonneaux d'allambique*". Lambic is old, a confusing, anachronistic relic of Brussels' pre-industrial age, even if its history does not stretch back as far as 500-year-old Bruegelian peasants.

Maybe, when Bruegel ventured into Brussels' pastoral hinterland, the workworn peasants and collapsed drunkards he found were drinking two beers that le Mercier did mention - *Keute* (Kuyte) and *Houppe* (Hoppe). And maybe the wheat Bruegel's harvesters are gathering made its way into mash tuns to make these beers, and others with names like *Braspenning* and *Waeghbaert* - unfamiliar syllables to our ears, but instantly recognisable to Bruegel and his peasants.

A History of Brussels Beer in 50 Objects

#7

In Het Carosseken **inn sign**

1860

- Pub Life

It's 1680, and a man stands on Brussels' *Rue Des Bouchers*, Butcher's Street. Guilders rattle in his money pouch. He's got a thirst that needs slaking. Outside number 47 a sign features a carriage, two horses, and the words *In Het Carosseken* ("In the Small Carriage"). He enters the inn. Navigating pigshit, sawdust, and haggling tradesmen from the nearby leather market he finds a table. What he can drink isn't something he has much control over. But neither does the innkeeper come to serve him, nor the brewer supplying the *Carosseken*. 17th century Brussels' real tastemakers are the tax collectors.

As a 1534 ordinance says, the city established rules "to remedy the great and manifold defects, complaints and irregularities that often happen….with beer in the city brewed, measured, and sold." The taxman's weapon against these defects was the *pegelstok*, a measuring stick that dictated the quantity of beer made from a fixed amount of malt and a variable volume of water. Historian Patricia Quintens, in *Bier en brouwerijen te Brussel*, explains:

> *"Every month the amount of beer changed,*

depending on the price of malt. The price of the beers themselves remained unchanged, only the "thickness" of the beer differed. If the grains were expensive, the beer "ran" somewhat "thinner". If cheaper, it was "thicker". Because each beer type had to be calculated with a specific pegel every time, the government limited the different beer types that could be brewed to what was strictly necessary.

The city also determined the amount and type of malt that could be used per brew. The volume of beer....that could be brewed from this malt was also determined by the city. This was calculated in such a way that the price of the beer and the profit for the brewer remain unchanged."

Before the finished beer was packaged, an official stuck his *pegelstok* into the vat to measure the final volume against notches corresponding to specific beers. If it reached the right notch, the beer was approved. Beers like *Waeghbaert*, made with six sisters of wheat (one sister equalled 48.7 litres), 11 of oats, and 18 amen water (one amen was 130 litres). *Hoppe* had a similar grain bill but brewed with 23 amen of water, resulting in a weaker beer. There was also *Roetbier* (red beer), *Zwartbier* (dark beer) and later *Dobbel* and *Braspenning* - the latter named for a coin worth a good workman's daily wages. If our Renaissance Brusselaar was adventurous he could choose a *Homborgen Bier* (Hamburg beer), *Oestbier* (Eastern beer), or something from the Baltics.

He plumps instead for a *Cuyte* (or *Kuyte/Kuit/Koyte*). A weaker, "small beer" made across the Low Countries with wheat, oats, and barley, he knows its reputation. Once stronger than *Waeghbaert*, people now complain it is little better than water. The excessive drunkenness it encourages will later inspire the expression *prendre une cuite* - "to get drunk". But one's enough for him, and anyway, his guilders only stretch so far at the *Carosseken*.

A History of Brussels Beer in 50 Objects

#8

Statue of Karel van Lotharingen

1705

- Business Life

"A more dreadful spectacle never was seen; nothing could more resemble what we are told of the burning of Troy" - James FitzJames, 1st Duke of Berwick

At 7pm on August 13, 1695, the skies above Brussels commenced to rain fire down on the city. French king Louis XIV, frustrated with the progress of his Nine Years' War, determined to make an example of Brussels. For three days the Sun King's troops pummeled the city with a barrage of cannonballs and firebombs, stopping only once, briefly, to reload. To keep their aim true they used the ornate spires of Brussels' Town Hall, on the Grand Place, as their target.

The bombardment ceased on August 15. A catastrophic fire ignited by the firebombing and stoked by Brussels' dense narrow streets and the wooden houses that crowded around them, which had raged for three days, subsided. All that was left of the Grand Place was shell-shocked facades looming over piles of rubble and ash, eliciting breathless comparisons to the sack of Troy. The buildings around the Town Hall were obliterated, including the one that used to stand at number 10: the *Maison de l'Arbre d'Or* ("House of the Golden

Tree"), known locally as the *Brauwershuys* and home to Brussels' brewers' guild.

The guild emerged in the 1400s, when it was officially recognised and admitted into a *nation*, one of nine umbrella bodies representing the city's artisan guilds. In the early 1600s they purchased the *l'Arbre d'Or* from the tapestry makers' guild to use as their headquarters, until the arrival of French cannonfire. But brewing was profitable, and the brewers' guild was wealthy. Within three years the guild had rebuilt *l'Arbre d'Or* as a gilded Baroque projection of influence. On the facade were reliefs of frolicking cherubs joining the harvests, hop picking and drinking beer, alongside columns decorated with hops and wheat.

In 1705 they mounted a grand equestrian statue on the roof. Maximilian II Emanuel, governor of the Spanish Netherlands, had failed to protect Brussels from destruction. But the brewers were canny politicians as well as successful businessmen and knew it wouldn't hurt to stroke the ego of a potential political patron. And when the political winds changed, they hauled Maximilian from his perch and replaced him with Karel van Lotharingen, the new governor of the now-*Austrian* Netherlands.

Karel is still there - though the current statue is a 1901 bronze replica of an 1852 replacement of the 1752 original - and the *l'Arbre d'Or* is largely unchanged since its reconstruction. The rest of the Grand Place was rebuilt too, the city's administrators taking advantage of the destruction to widen streets, improve sanitation, and demolish fire-prone buildings.

The 1695 bombardment was Brussels' first great urban calamity. It would not be the last, nor the last one to strike at the heart of the city's brewing fraternity. The next great upheaval of Brussels' urban fabric wouldn't come from foreign invaders but from the reconstructed towers of the next-door Town Hall that overshadow Karel's gleaming bronze steed.

EEDT

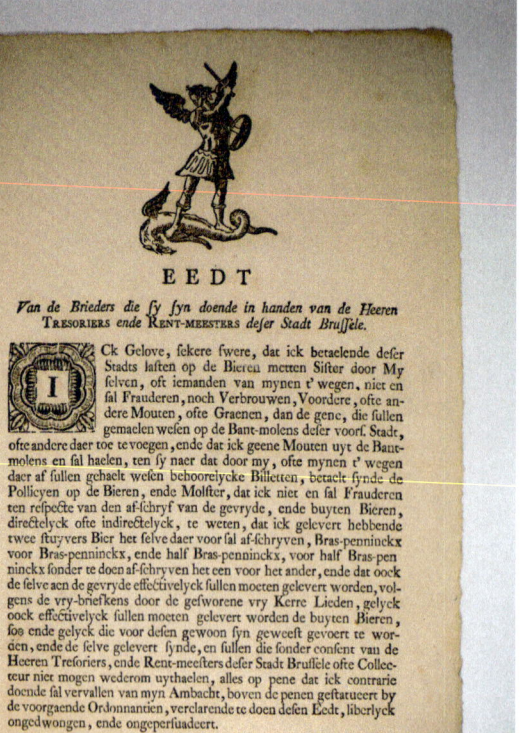

Van de Brieders die sy syn doende in handen van de Heeren
Tresoriers *ende* Rent-Meesters *deser Stadt Brussele.*

Ck Gelove, sekere swere, dat ick betaelende deser Stadts lasten op de Bieren metten Sister door My selven, oft iemanden van mynen t' wegen, niet en sal Frauderen, noch Verbrouwen, Voordere, ofte andere Mouten, ofte Graenen, dan de gene, die sullen gemaelen wesen op de Bant-molens deser voorss. Stadt, ofte andere daer toe te voegen, ende dat ick geene Mouten uyt de Bant-molens en sal haelen, ten sy naer dat door my, ofte mynen t' wegen daer af sullen gehaelt wesen behoorelycke Billetten, betaelt synde de Pollicyen op de Bieren, ende Molster, dat ick niet en sal Frauderen ten respecte van den af-schryf van de gevryde, ende buyten Bieren, directelyck ofte indirectelyck, te weten, dat ick gelevert hebbende twee stuyvers Bier het selve daer voor sal af-schryven, Bras-penninckx voor Bras-penninckx, ende half Bras-penninckx, voor half Bras-pen ninckx sonder te doen af-schryven het een voor het ander, ende dat oock de selve aen de gevryde effectivelyck sullen moeten gelevert worden, volgens de vry-briefkens door de gesworene vry Kerre Lieden, gelyck oock effectivelyck sullen moeten gelevert worden de buyten Bieren, soo ende gelyck die voor desen gewoon syn geweest gevoert te worden, ende de selve gelevert synde, en sullen die sonder consent van de Heeren Tresoriers, ende Rent-meesters deser Stadt Brussele ofte Collecteur niet mogen wederom uythaelen, alles op pene dat ick contrarie doende sal vervallen van myn Ambacht, boven de penen gestatueert by de voorgaende Ordonnantien, verclarende te doen desen Eedt, liberlyck ongedwongen, ende ongepersuadeert.

ALSOO MOET MY GODT HELPEN ENDE ALLE SYNE HEYLIGHEN.

#9

Brewers' Oath

1750

- Business Life

"Oath for the brewers who put their work in the hands of the Treasurers and Stewards of this City of Brussels..."

So begins a brewers' (*Brieders* in the local dialect) oath published in 1750. It committed members of Brussels' brewers' guild to pay tax, to not act fraudulently, to use only grain from Brussels' mills, to brew and deliver beer that was ordered of them, and to settle their debts. Failure to do so meant expulsion from the guild and serious financial penalties. In truth, the oath was honoured more in its breach than its observance.

The brewers' guild, like all of Brussels' medieval artisan guilds, was a monopoly, a position they leveraged for self-enrichment. They also used it to occasionally flex political influence, having - alongside the other guilds - been granted consultative input into Brussels' governance in 1421. Each guild was a member of a *nation*, a grouping of similar trades; brewers were part of the St. Jacques *nation* alongside bakers and pastry bakers, millers, coopers, cabinetmakers, tilers and wine traders. As well as the right to a say on administrative matters, the guild used their monopoly position to determine the quality, quantity and price of raw materials, the price of beer, the way it was brewed, and how it was sold.

Beer was popular, and the brewers' guild became a wealthy and powerful institution. They were, for example, invited to participate in the processional welcomes of visiting royals, sending on one occasion 30 torchbearers to meet Eleanor of Austria (compared to a measly 18 bakers). And when the Coudenberg palace burnt down in 1731, the brewers generously offered to finance its reconstruction, with one proviso: Brussels would abolish beer taxes. The city refused, disinclined to miss out on 190,000 *florins* of annual brewing tax income.

But city officials did recognise an entrenched vested interest when they saw one, and occasionally attempted corrective measures to bring them to heel. Brussels' Treasurers periodically published edicts abolishing the guild's monopoly on brewing, only for its members to down tools altogether. In one instance in 1655, after Town Hall administrators had proclaimed the expulsion of the brewers' guild from their *nation*, brewers blockaded mills, harassed excise collectors, issued death threats to city aldermen, and pelted magistrates with cobblestones.

Order was eventually restored, and the delicate balance between oath-breaking brewers and their counterparts in Brussels' tax collection offices, continued throughout the 1700s. That is, until it came to an abrupt end right at the end of that century.

French revolutionary troops entered Brussels on July 11, 1795, and four months later on November 10, they extended France's *Loi d'Allard* to the territories of the now-dissolved Austrian Netherlands: the all-powerful guilds - brewers included - were stripped of their monopolies and dissolved. Henceforth, anyone in Brussels had the right to brew beer. The guildhalls were expropriated and sold off a year later, and it would be more than 150 years before the brewers' guild Maison des Brasseurs would echo again to the chatter of haggling brewers.

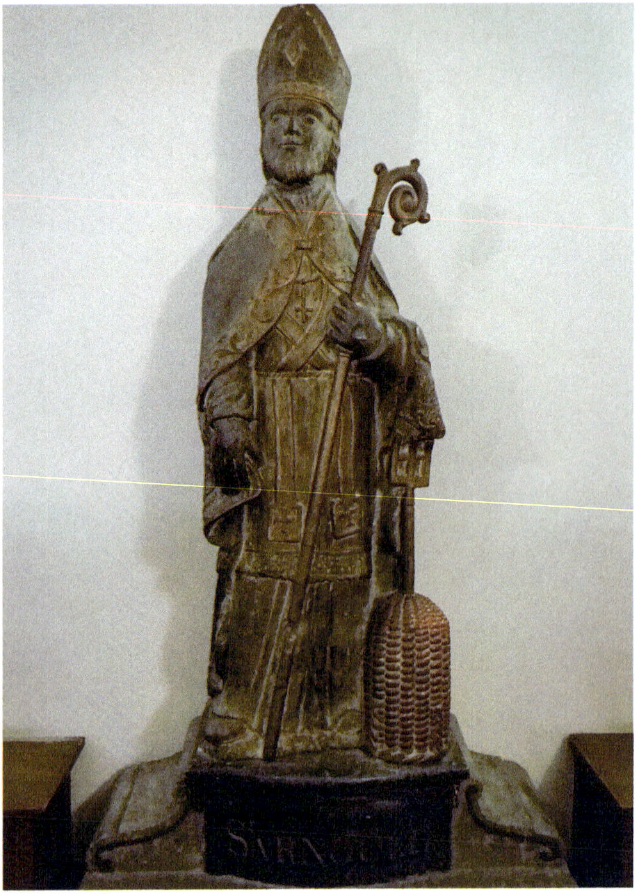

A History of Brussels Beer in 50 Objects

#10

Statue of St. Arnoldus

1700s

- Business Life

The life of an 18th century Brussels brewer was a comfortable one. A lucrative monopoly on brewing, political influence and prestige, and the willingness to use it. But to secure these privileges you first had to make it into the brewers' guild, which meant becoming a master brewer. That cost time, money, and connections.

First, there was a two-year apprenticeship alongside an existing master brewer. This, and guild membership, cost money. The son of an established brewer was expected to pay 13 guilders, the son of a future brewer 400, and for everyone else 1,000. For 2,000 guilders aspirant brewers could skip the apprenticeship stage. Most brewers in this era rented their brewery from a fellow guild member, which could cost up to 900 guilders annually. A delivery horse might set you back another 2,000. These costs, and the guild's desire to suppress numbers to ensure there was enough business for everyone, kept numbers low; in 1658 there were 80 guild members, and 94 in 1678.

Temporal dues paid, new arrivals to the brewer's stately Grand Place guildhall might consider giving spiritual thanks to their new patron saint, Arnold of Soissons.

Arnold (or *Arnoldus*) was born near Oudenaarde around 1040. Originally a soldier, he became a monk and eventually bishop of Soissons, in northern France. He is remembered by brewers for brewing while abbot of St. Peter's Abbey in Oudenburg, and for his rescuing of local peasants from a deadly infectious disease outbreak by enticing them to drink beer instead of contaminated water. For this, Arnold is usually depicted clutching a brewer's mash paddle - like this 1768 statue from a brewery in Soignies.

Unfortunately, Arnold failed to intercede in defence of guild members when they needed him, as in 1795 when French revolutionary troops dissolved the guild, ended its monopoly and evicted them from the Grand Place. It was 1951 when they finally returned as tenants of the Maison des Brasseurs. Arnold came with them. In a first floor meeting room, where their antecedents had met for guild business, this new generation of brewers installed stained glass windows featuring the abbot wreathed in beer jugs, brewing baskets and beer barrels, and performing miracles surrounded by beer-swilling angels. His statue became part of a museum in the cellar, and Arnold's feast day (August 14) was revived as a central part of the activities of the newly-created Order of the Knights of the Brewers' Paddle. An evocation of the guild days of old - though now extended to the whole country - the Order was a business-cum-social club for active and retired brewers.

Every year, on the last Friday in August, knights in their flowing red robes and polished medallions trek from the Maison des Brasseurs to Brussels' cathedral on the Treurenberg to pay homage to their patron saint, returning to the Grand Place to induct new knights and, in the presence of the great and good from Belgian beer, tap the first ceremonial keg of the Belgian Beer Weekend festival.

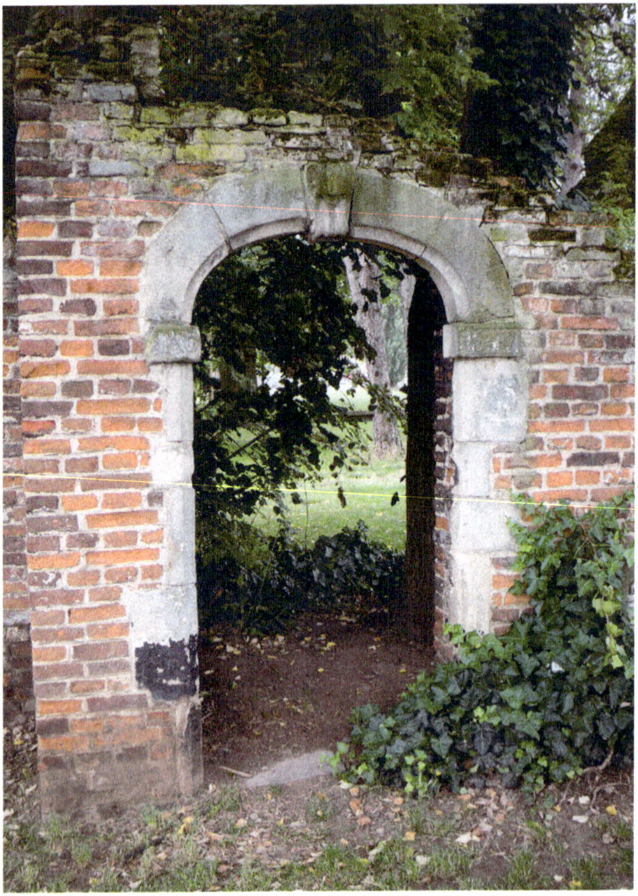

#11

Entrance to Het Heideken

1647

- Pub Life

Taverne. Auberge. Assommoir. Early-19th century Brussels did not want for drinking dens, prime among them medieval inns that had evolved into *cabarets*. Not Liza Minelli-haunted, Nazi-satirizing theatres but dimly-lit, sparsely furnished establishments for the city's working men to slip into for a draw on their pipe and a tankard of *Cuyte*. Writing in the 1880s, Brussels-born Camille Lemonnier captured the mood of the Brussels cabaret:

> *"....almost all of them extend in a narrow passage under a low ceiling, varnished by smoke, with a corner for the counter; the largest would hold barely thirty people....The sink, the kitchen, the room lie on the same plane, through a mist of vapors rising from the pots; and the smell of the stoves spreads among the customers, in hot and continual puffs. No coquetry of crockery or silverware either; plates are placed in front of you, with pewter cutlery, on a rough napkin; the public is seen by the caterer as a working machine that does not need tempting by refinements."*

Someone seeking fresh air and respite from the oppressive city might make for an out-of-town cabaret in Brussels' agricultural hinterland. Villages like Hembeek, Watermael, and Boondael were long a destination for city residents yearning for some greenery and a good beer. Out beyond the city walls, cabarets doubled as inns, breweries, creameries, and farms. Places like Uccle's Misverstand, Jette's Ferme de Wilg, or Het Heideken in Ganshoren.

Originally a farm, the Heideken had evolved by the 1800s into an all-purpose *auberge-ferme*. It comprised two buildings - a sagging white cottage and a more upright red-bricked building - corralled by a small terrace and facing onto a large green. Stamped on the redbrick building's arched white stone entrance was the Heideken's construction date, 1647. In the courtyard, chickens pecked grain from between uneven cobblestones. Inside, the floors were of bare wood, on the walls shelves of crockery and small, framed portraits. Cabinets stacked with glassware stood behind a small bar, and rags hung drying before the fireplace.

Around wooden chairs and small tables, customers tucked into glasses of Lambic and plates of *tartine au fromage blanc*. Like many of its contemporaries, the Heideken was a centre of communal life. It hosted the local archery club, who practised on the green. Local artist circles met there, sharing tables with members of Ganshoren's municipal council who used the Heideken as an ersatz town hall in the absence of a real one.

And like many of its contemporaries, the Heideken was unable to resist a fast-encroaching and rapidly-suburbanising city that was absorbing the rural villages on its edge. Brussels subsumed Ganshoren in 1954, but by then the Heideken and its centuries-old bucolic tableau had been obliterated, the cabaret demolished to make way for a new suburban tram.

All that remains of the Heideken is its name on a nearby street and its stone entrance. Salvaged and repurposed, the white archway now stands forgotten and moss-rotten under a yawning willow tree, a memorial to the neighbourhood's vanished rural past.

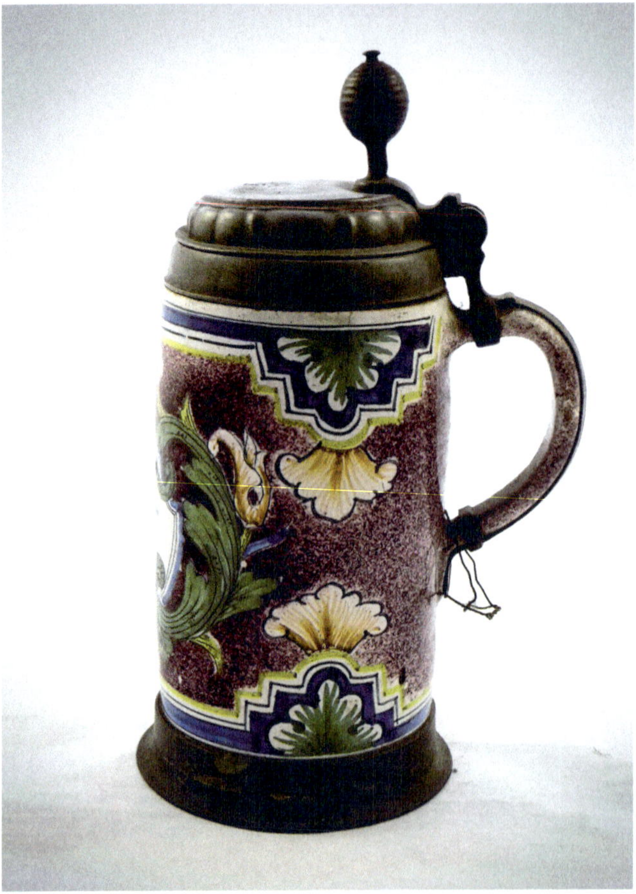

#12
Bierkruk
1765

- City Life

As 1799 ticked over into 1800, Brussels was stepping out from the old world and into a new one. The *ancièn regime* of the Austrian Hapsburgs had been swept away by a whirlwind of revolutionary troops from France. The Zenne river, on the banks of which *Bruocsella* was born 800 years previously, was no longer all-powerful. Its marshy floodplain was drained and put to productive use, sowed with crops and set aside as drying fields for the tanners and cloth merchants.

Centuries of tinkering with the river's flow and course had resulted in a patchwork inner city of islands and bridges, with mills built on the river's edge to harness its meagre energy. Already by mid-millennium the river was usurped as Brussels' connection to the outside world by the digging of a canal to Willebroek, stretching from the city's fish market to the outer reaches of Antwerp and eventually to the lucrative maritime trade on the North Sea coast.

Even before French troops entered the city in 1795 Brussels' political power was at a low ebb, its apogee as the imperial capital of Charles V's globe spanning empire long past. The Coudenberg palace, where

Keizer Karel abdicated in 1556, was reduced to an ashy ruin in 1731. Charles' Spanish inheritors had also vanished, ceding Brussels to their Austrian Hapsburg cousins and ushering in a short century of enlightened absolutist rule directed remotely from the Hofburg in Vienna.

Brussels remained beholden to the demands of its sclerotic artisan guilds, constantly fighting the attempts by Austrian governors to introduce modernising economic reforms. The city remained an important transit point on regional trade routes, for example receiving wine from France to the west, and shipping it on eastward to The Netherlands and Germany to the east.

Lace and porcelain makers continued to ply their wares with the favour of the court, alongside more everyday activities like brewing, tanning, textiles, soap-making, sugar and salt refineries, and paper factories clogging the city streets and fouling the Zenne. Turn of the century beer drinkers in the Heideken or any other of the city's many taverns and *cabarets* would have been intimately familiar with the output of Brussels' potters. Just like Charles himself, who gave pride of place to his four-handled beer mug, the earthenware tankard was the drinking vessel of choice for the *Bruxellois*. Brussels' *faïence* factories concentrated on the production of utilitarian ceramics for an emerging bourgeois *clientèle*.

Some, like this 1765 *bierkruk*, were brightly-couloured with floral motifs. Others featured pastoral drinking scenes, and yet more were more sober, more Teutonic, in their design.

There would be more political upheaval to come, as the end of the Napoleonic Wars 15 years into the new 19th century brought Brussels under the control of a new set of sober Dutch sovereigns. Presumably they too, like their predecessors, were ready with their own ceramic beer mugs, eager to fill them with Lambic, Faro, Uytzet, Peeterman, Hoegaerds, Diestse, and whatever other beers Brussels' 19th century taverns were ready to provide.

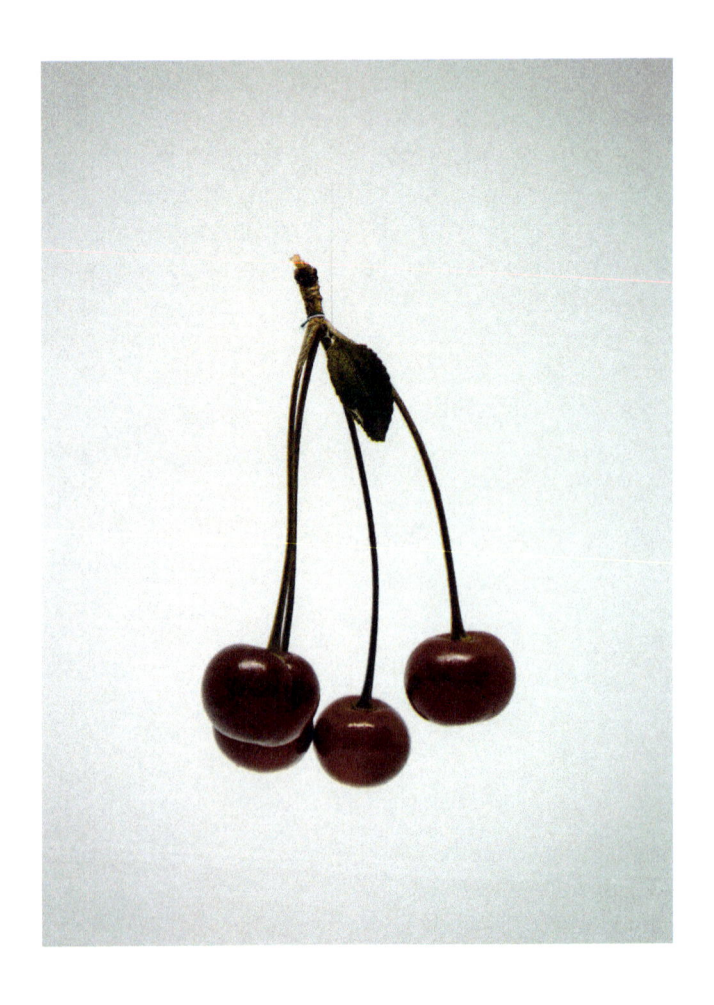

#13

Schaarbeekse Kriek

1700s (harvested July 2021)

- Farm Life

Schaarbeek is famous for two things: donkeys and cherries. The Brussels municipality, now largely residential, was once farmland. From the 12th century, donkeys (*ezels* in Dutch) were driven down the *Ezelweg* road, carrying produce for central Brussels' food markets. The clacking of their hooves on cobblestone streets caused the people living there to shout *"Daar zijn de ezels van Schaarbeek!"* - "There go Schaarbeek's donkeys!" Schaarbeek was the *Ezelstad*, Donkey Town, and its residents nicknamed *ezels*.

These ezels often carried baskets of *Prunus cerasus* "*Schaarbeekse Kriek*" - small, dark, sour Morello cherries, destined for use by Brussels' brewers. This relationship between Schaarbeek cherry farmer and Brussels brewer was sufficiently established as far back as 1792 for the Belgian nobleman Philippe d'Olmen de Poederlé, in his *Manuel de l'Arboriste et du Forestier Belgique*, to remark: "[a]mong the cherries grown in the village of Scharbeck....we see many of the cherry trees that its inhabitants come to sell....to our brewers, and for the most part, their *Swarte-Kriecken*."

Throughout the 19th century Schaarbeekse Krieken

were used by brewers from Brussels and the Zenne valley to make ruby-red *Kriekenlambiek*, or *Kriek Lambic,* or just *Kriek*. A 1907 article, unearthed by *Hors Catégorie Brewing's* Dave Janssen, loosely describes the process. Brewers preferred whole, fresh cherries, using 160-200 grams for every litre of beer. The Lambic they used was a blend of different vintages - 20% three-year-old, 50% two-year-old and 30% one-year-old. Aged in barrels for four or five months, the Kriek was then bottle conditioned for another six before release, after which it could keep its condition for up to five years.

But by 1907 the demographic upheaval that would obliterate the Schaarbeekse Kriek was already underway. Schaarbeek's population grew from 6,211 in 1846, to 63,500 in 1900, ballooning to 123,000 by 1946. Rapid urbanisation ate into the land occupied by cherry orchards, and by the end of the 20th century the Schaarbeekse Kriek had slipped inexorably into folklore. It was remembered only in stained glass windows in the town hall, cherry blossoms on the avenues around *Plaskyplein*, and at *Square des Griottiers*, named after the cherry harvest workers.

But rumours of the death of the Schaarbeek cherry were premature. It survived outside Brussels in the Zenne valley, where brewers sporadically used the fruit to make Kriek (when they weren't using Gorsem cherries or fruit sourced from Poland). Eventually, Kriek producers like 3 Fonteinen and Oud Beersel began planting their own orchards. This revival had already reached Brussels in 2011, when a coalition of cultural organisations and tree-planting advocates called the Bûûmplanters began planting Schaarbeekse Kriek trees in the gardens of Schaarbeek residents.

In 2018, Brasserie Cantillon planted their own patch of cherry trees at a cooperative farm in Anderlecht. And in 2021 the Bûûmplanters were able to produce 10kg of cherries. Enough for Schaarbeek's own, newly-opened Brasserie de la Mule to brew a Schaarbeekse Kriek beer, 500 metres from the old *Ezelweg* that once echoed to the clopping hooves of Schaarbeekse *ezels*.

A History of Brussels Beer in 50 Objects

#14

Lambikstoemper

1800s

- Pub Life

"'t gaat regenen, 't gaat regenen, 't gaat regenen dat het giet, en als wij geene Faro hebben dan drinken wij Lambiek."

"It's going to rain, it's going to rain, it's going to pour, and if we don't have Faro, we'll drink Lambic."

The children singing this ditty knew the natural order of Brussels' beer hierarchy. Faro first. Lambic second, and everything else in the ha'penny place. Where the latter was tart, cloudy, and funky, Faro was sweet and light, a workhorse of a beer popular with the men, women and children of early-19th century Brussels. That sweetness came from the addition of sugar, often served alongside the beer and requiring the use of a slim metal implement ubiquitous in Belgian taverns in the 1800s, a loop on one end and a flattened disc on the other: the *lambikstoemper*.

The first written mention of Faro - in a 1721 description of a bacchanalia alongside *"Leuvens bier...Liersche kaves, Hoegaerts en diergelyke Sorbetten der Dronkaarts"* - predates Lambic. But the histories of these two beers were closely intertwined, if slightly clouded by Lambic history's usual mythomania. The Faro of the 19th century was usually a 50-50 blend of aged Lambic and a beer called *Meerts* or *Bière de Mars*, a weaker Lambic byproduct. It was defined by the addition of sugar, typically procured from Belgium's booming sugar beet industry. Sometimes blended by a beer merchant, who might also add sugar and deliver a pre-sweetened Faro, often the blending and sweetening was left to the tavern-owners. They would hand their customer a mug of Faro, a sugar cube, and a lambikstoemper, and invite them to mash the sugar into the bottom of their tankard, lending Faro its characteristic sweetness.

It was Faro's softer profile - and lower ABV - which likely explains its success in Brussels and beyond, the beer reaching Leuven, The Netherlands, and Paris. Described contemporaneously as "*moelleuse, gaillarde, et faraude*" ("mellow, cheerful, and tawny"), Faro earned the nickname "liqueur d'or", as well as comparisons to wine from the eponymous Portuguese city (all mooted origins of the name). But Faro's ubiquity in Brussels did not mean ubiquitous popularity. Charles Baudelaire, in the syphilitic delirium of his final days in debtor's exile in Brussels, disagreed with his Parisian compatriots on Faro's qualities, cursing it as a "synonym" for urine, brewed with - and tasting of - human effluent dumped into the Zenne river.

He may have scorned the lambikstoemper, but Baudelaire's literary contemporaries were less caustic. As the characters in William Thackeray's novel *Vanity Fair* decamp to Brussels on the eve of 1815's Battle of Waterloo, Thackeray turns to beer when seeking to sketch out the Belgian locals. The insolent manservant Monsieur Isidor, idly tending to his English master, daydreams of "rambling along the Green Avenue, dressed out in a frogged coat….examining the barges sailing slowly under the cool shadows of the trees by the canal, or refreshing himself with a mug of Faro at the bench of a beer-house on the road to Laeken."

MATHYS-PETIGNIOT
Md de bières
RUE DU MIROIR
6
JETTE St.PIERRE

#15

Bottletop, marchand de bières

1800s

- Business Life

On May 3, 1867, a small notice appeared on the *Journal de Bruxelles* back page. Printed alongside advertisements for chocolate and hotels, it announced the sale of assets of a business on the Rue des Teinturiers:

1,000 barrels of excellent Lambic, Faro, and Mars beer, a portion of empty barrels and of hops, and the utensils of a marchand de bières.

The *marchand de bières* ("beer merchant") was, historian Martine De Keukeleire says, one of four key actors in 19th century Brussels' beer industry. Maltsters made malt, brewers turned it into beer, which *cabaret* owners served. But between brewery and *cabaretier* came the *marchand de bières* (also called *préperateur*, or *apprêteur*).

The merchant's job was to source Lambic and Mars beer from breweries, blend and condition it at their own warehouse for sale to cabarets and taverns. Sometimes merchants - "brewers without breweries" - commissioned breweries to make their beer. Others, described as *"grands connaisseurs"* - visited local breweries to source the best Lambics and Mars beers already in barrel.

However they sourced their base beers, the merchants then sweetened it, coloured it, clarified it, and packaged it as Faro, *petit Faro*, and table beer. To differentiate themselves from brewers, merchants might etch their names onto bottles or stamp it on bottle tops, like this example from Mathys-Petigniot, a *marchand de bières* from Jette.

Beer merchants weren't always distinguishable from breweries. In 1822, Brussels did not make a distinction between the two, listing no *marchand de bières* in their annual business almanach. Breweries may have functioned as both, running, as historian Lucas Catherine describes, *voortappen* - where you could sit and drink - and *tappen*, shops that sold beer at various measurements, starting at the half litre. But by 1834 the number of standalone beer merchants had reached five.

By 1866 - a year before the liquidation of the business on Rue Des Teinturiers - Brussels' business directory counted 100 *Marchand en gros de bières indigènes et étrangères* ("Wholesale merchants of local and foreign beer"). Such was the beer merchants' success, and such was the need for space to store barrels of Lambic and other beers for up to three years of barrel-conditioning, that at one point in the 19th century beer warehouses made up 75% of the total warehouse space in central Brussels.

That list from 1866 is testament to the fact that the distinction between brewery and beer merchant remained ambiguous, featuring as it did a brewery like Wielemans-Ceuppens - then still located in the Marolles neighbourhood but on the verge of a move to a modern, purpose-built brewery in Vorst. And as the name of the category into which the city allotted them indicated, beer merchants had branched out from Lambic. From the 1850s onwards, Brussels' drinkers had begun to get a taste for foreign beers, and beer merchants were keen to milk this growing market. By 1897, alongside the traditional listings for Lambic *préperateurs* and *apprêteurs* were mentions of Bass & Co. Pale Ale and Bavarian Löwenbrau, and large illustrations for Allsopp's Stout Impériel.

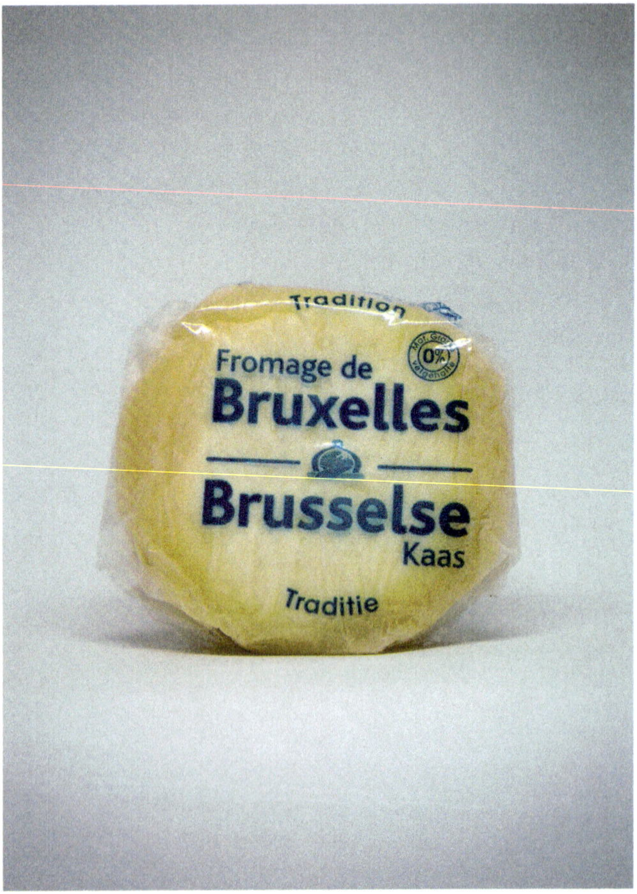
Tradition
Fromage de
Bruxelles
Brusselse
Kaas
Traditie

#16
Fromage de Bruxelles
1800s

- Farm Life

Plattekaas. Mandjeskaas. Ettekees. Pottekees. Kaas - cheese - has always been a staple of Brussels' drinking culture. Not the sweaty blocks of yellow rubber, doused in celery salt or dijon mustard, that we know today, but characterful, singe-your-nostril-hair strong cheeses, "children of the Payottenland" made by farmers from nearby villages in the Zenne valley. *Plattekaas* was a 19th century favourite, a smooth and spreadable quark-style cheese served with a dense slice of *boerenbrood* ("farmer's bread"), topped with thick slivers of locally-grown *Ramonaches* (radishes) and washed down with a glass of Faro in a roadside inn on Brussels' rural outskirts.

Mandjeskaas ("basket cheese"), similar to plattekaas and cultured in retired Lambic barrels, earned its name from the wicker baskets in which the curds were traditionally drained. *Ettekees*, or *Ettekeis* or *Hettekees*, was a true Brussels cheese - hence its French name, *Fromage de Bruxelles*. Made with low-fat cow's milk, ettekees is matured for two-to-four months, washed with salty water, and brined. Hard (*hette*) where plattekaas was soft, it is salty and tart and with a meaty aroma - pungent enough to become a nickname for

Brussels' small neighbourhood cinemas thanks to their odorific similarities.

To soften ettekees' harder aromatic edges, it was mixed with plattekaas, a shallot, and the occasional "seasoning" of Lambic or Faro and christened *Pottekees* (or *pottekeis*). Lambic (or Faro or Geuze) was not only an ingredient in pottekees but considered the drink that accompanied it best, the reasons for which a 1915 newspaper report makes clear: "the slightly heady beer helps the stomach to digest the pottekees, and pottekees helps the stomach to withstand this slightly heady beer with impunity."

The culinary world from which pottekees emerged was not a gilded one. Like the other 19th century Brussels classics - *tête pressée* (head cheese), *bloempanch* (pork blood sausage), and *choesels* (madeira-soaked bovine offcuts - the pancreas, but also testicles, intestines, and other, lesser organs) - pottekees was *volksvoedsel* ("folk food") made and consumed by the city's lower classes.

When a better-off middle class emerged in the late 1800s, they wanted to socialise in glass palaces, drink foreign beers, and jettison the ripe cheese that marked them out as proletarian. When, in 1876, debauched author Joris-Karl Huysmans detailed a lavish spread at a Grand Place brasserie he mentioned Lambic and Faro, *pistolets* with butter, crab entrails in green sauce, and smoked eel. But no *Fromage de Bruxelles*, and no pottekees.

But pottekees was not eradicated completely, surviving in the city's food markets and in the taverns and cabarets hidden in the narrow alleyways sheltering by the Grand Place. In World War I it was rationed, 80 centimes getting a hungry Brussellaar a 100g portion. It survived WWII too, and by the 1970s there were still chefs in the *Îlot Sacré* making traditional pottekees. Mandjeskaas and Fromage de Bruxelles was delivered by a ruddy, beret-wearing cheesemonger. The cheese mashed together, peppered and salted, sprinkled with shallots, and irrigated with a little milk. Spread onto *boerenbrood* and washed down with a "Santeï!" and a slurp of russet-hued Geuze.

A History of Brussels Beer in 50 Objects

#17

Zagemanneke

1800s

- Pub Life

There's always one. The droning know it all. The bloviating self-promoter. The mean drunk wheedling their way from conversation to conflict. The pub loudmouth is a familiar archetype, but the owners of Brussels' 19th century drinking establishments knew how to handle them. If the signs stuck above the bar enjoining customers not to swear failed, these *cafébazen* had another, more whimsical weapon in their arsenal.

They would place a marionette with a narrow stand - wooden or metal, with a red nose and workman's attire - on the bar's edge. A curved saw or metal sheet protruded from the marionette, arcing below the countertop and weighted at the end. Confronted with a whining drinker, or sensing an impending conflagration between customers, the barman would tap the head of the marionette. It would commence see-sawing, indicating to the querulous drinkers that their behaviour was repetitive, tiresome and unwanted. This was the *Zagemanneke* - meaning both "Sawing Man" and "Complaining Man", *zagen* being the shared Flemish word for these discrete activities.

The Zagemanneke was a familiar feature of Brussels'

19th century *estaminets* - successors of the city's 18th century inns, taverns, and cabarets. Estaminet as a word is classic Brussels *patois*, its meaning found either in the bastardisation of the Spanish for "just a minute". Or the corruption of the barked enticements of Flemish-speaking barmen to drinkers seeking seclusion for philanderous liaisons. Or an evolution of the Wallonian colloquialism *en stam* ("with family"), estaminets being popular venues for family occasions.

Whatever estaminet's etymology, it was well-established by the 1810s. By 1862, one guidebook counted 1,679 Brussels estaminets - places like *Le Jardin Joyeaux* ("Happy Garden") on the Vlaamsesteenweg, *In 't Spinnekopke* on the Bloemenhofplein, or *Au Coin du Diable* ("The Devil's Corner"), which, folklorist Robert Desart wrote, housed "a black wooden statuette with golden horns and red velvet coat."

The estaminet was better-lit, its décor less shabby, and the food better than the drinking establishments of previous centuries. There was Lambic and Faro, but also wheat beers from Brabant, provincial *bières brunes*, and later English Pale Ales and German Lager served through intricately-detailed ceramic beer engines.

They were modest operations though, designed for drinking and smoking. Writing in 1888, Camille Lemonnier praised their "rudimentary simplicity….any distraction that could disturb the customer's tasting of fermented liquid is ruled out as prejudicial to the seriousness of this occupation". He particularly valued the estaminet's role as a place where people - men - could socialise relatively unhindered by traditional class boundaries:

"...[W]e frequently meet around tables....husbands who have just buried their wives, businessmen suffering the blow of a financial disaster, the doctor, the lawyer, judges, the civil servant....as well as the small shopkeeper and the mason....an equality of all classes in the smoky tobacco shop, where twelve centimes can buy the poor and the rich a warm place....and the freedom to rail against the Jesuits, the *gendarmes*, and power".

Just as long as these personal declamations or anti-establishment tirades did not incur the Zagemanneke's wrath.

GRANDE·BRASSERIE·DE·KOEKELBERG
lez Bruxelles
Société Anonyme
Fabrique
BOCK
Concessionnaires au Littoral
FEYS FRÈRES Ostende

#18
Koekelberg Bock Beer
1887

- Brewery Life

On May 3 1887, Brussels was alerted to an important event happening two days hence on the city's Koekelberg plateau. In an advert occupying a quarter of the back page of three local newspapers were the words, in bold type, **MUNICH** and **BOCK**, "brewed exactly like the more celebrated beers of Munich, conceding nothing in terms of quality and taste….made only with the best malts and finest hops." In even bolder print above this was printed: *Brasserie de Bières Allemands de Koekelberg*. The notice announced the Koekelberg brewery's big opening, and its owner's conviction that a market in Brussels existed for locally-made Lager beers.

Foreign beers were scarce in early-19th century Brussels, but by the 1850s estaminets were advertising their stock of "Pale Ale - *le véritable bière anglaise*" and *bières de bavières*. Two decades later, the popularity of German beer was such that industry figures argued in the letter pages of national newspapers about whether Belgian breweries could - or should - brew Bavarian beers. On one side were Belgian brewers wanting to exploit the domestic appetite for *Mitteleuropa* Lagers, but felt Belgium's excise regime prevented them. Opposing them was Adolphe Frentz, editor of industry periodical *Le Moniteur de la Brasserie*, who argued that the taxes were not the problem:

"[R]eal Bavarian beer....can only be brewed in Bavaria. That which is brewed here....is only an imitation....The clientele - composed for the most part of foreigners - who consume these exotic beers, will never entirely give up on sourcing them from their own countries. [Why not?] Patriotism for some; for others, an innate bias against local products. For many, a hint of vanity."

For Frentz, imported beer was a small market - 40,000 hectoliters in 1871 compared to 10 million hectoliters of Belgian beer. But by 1910, Belgium would be importing 237,000 hectolitres of "exotic beer" annually. Despite Frentz's scorn, Koekelberg's German brewers reckoned they could persuade a portion of these drinkers to buy Brussels-brewed *Bockbier*.

And so, in May 1887, director Edouard Köller welcomed 4,000 visitors for the brewery's grand unveiling, serving 4,500 litres of freshly-tapped beer. Guests marvelled at the artificial ice-maker, the machine room's steam-clouded pistons, and the brewery cellar's "monstrous" wooden foeders, nostrils overwhelmed by the smell of oak and fermenting beer. That first year, Koekelberg brewed 3,140 hectolitres of Bavarian beer. Within five years Koekelberg exceeded their original 50,000 hectolitre capacity, and in 1900 churned out 53,778 hectolitres of Bock, Munich, and Petit Bavière.

But Köller's ambition was bigger than just supplying Brussels' estaminets and cafés. The brewery's *Munich Hähnebrau* won a gold medal at a competition in

Munich in 1898, causing Bavarian brewers to cry foul about the beer's authenticity, affronted by a Belgian brewery appropriating the word "Munich". By then, the brewery had also changed its name. *Brasserie de Bières Allemands* was gone. Instead, the *Grande Brasserie de Koekelberg* was ready to welcome a 20th century wherein Brussels' irrepressible obsession with all things German would continue, unhindered.

FOR
WIELEMANS
CEUPPENS.
BY THE
DE LA VERGNE
REFRIGERATING
MACHINE COMPANY,
NEW YORK.
1894.

#19

De La Vergne Compressor

1894

- Brewery Life

Only the best would do for brothers Prosper, Edouard, and André Wielemans. Born of brewing stock (father a beer merchant, grandfather a brewer), the boys joined their widowed mother Constance-Ida Ceuppens in the family trade in the 1870s, converting their father's merchant business into a brewery. Finding success brewing local styles, in 1879 the boys and their mother uprooted the Wielemans-Ceuppens brewery from its home in downtown Brussels in search of room to grow and diversify.

Centrifugal forces - the razing of central Brussels during the burial of the Zenne, the pressures of industrialisation, and the city's dense urban squalor - scattered breweries like Wielemans from Brussels' medieval core to its rapidly-industrialising periphery. Some breweries landed in Molenbeek. The Wielemans headed for Vorst, where land was cheap, plentiful and beside the railway and the canal.

Escaping their origins in Brussels' medieval core, these breweries also shed their artisanal traditions, abandoning Lambic in favour of industrial-scale Bavarian-style Lager beers. Wielemans-Ceuppens were no different, but as they shifted in the 1880s from spontaneous fermentation to bottom-fermented Lager, they found their new brewery was not up to the job. So the brothers went in search of something better: a new, German-built brewhouse, and a Bavarian brewmaster from Würzburg to run it.

In October 1887, Wielemans-Ceuppens released their first *Bavière* and *Petite-Bavière*. The beers were successful, securing medals and drinkers, but the brothers remained dissatisfied. Popularity meant increased demand for their beer. Which put pressure on the brewery's artificial cooling system - providing the cold ambient cellar temperatures their *Bavière* needed while lagering in 400 50-hectolitre wooden barrels. Their German system could not cope, so the brothers went looking for something better. Not to Germany, but an engineering firm on the banks of the Harlem river in The Bronx.

New York's De La Vergne Engineering Company built for the Wielemans a steam-powered, wrought iron compressor. Four metres tall, it comprised two three metre-wide wheels and two vertical pistons. It was a unique piece of industrial engineering, absorbing fully half the brewery's budget for their brewery upgrade. The Wielemans installed it in a new, brewhouse-adjacent machine room decorated with geometric tiling and beer-themed stained glass. Collectively, the De La Vergne and the other machines produced 750,000 *frigories* an hour. Enough *frigories* to keep the Wielemans' beers sufficiently chilled.

Steam power was soon jettisoned for first coal and then electricity, and by the 1920s even New York's finest could not satisfy Wielemans-Ceuppens' demand for cold air. The De La Vergne compressor was replaced but stayed put, unused, for six decades. It stayed put when the brewery closed in 1989. And it stayed put when the machine room was abandoned, though its black paintwork rusted, its wheels seized, and its brass balustrades dulled.

Rescued by industrial heritage preservationists, the compressor still stands where Prosper, Edouard and André left it. Embossed lettering on the side of the machine still proclaims, in newly-painted gold: "Built and erected for Wielemans Ceuppens by the De La Vergne Refrigerating Machine Company, New York, 1894".

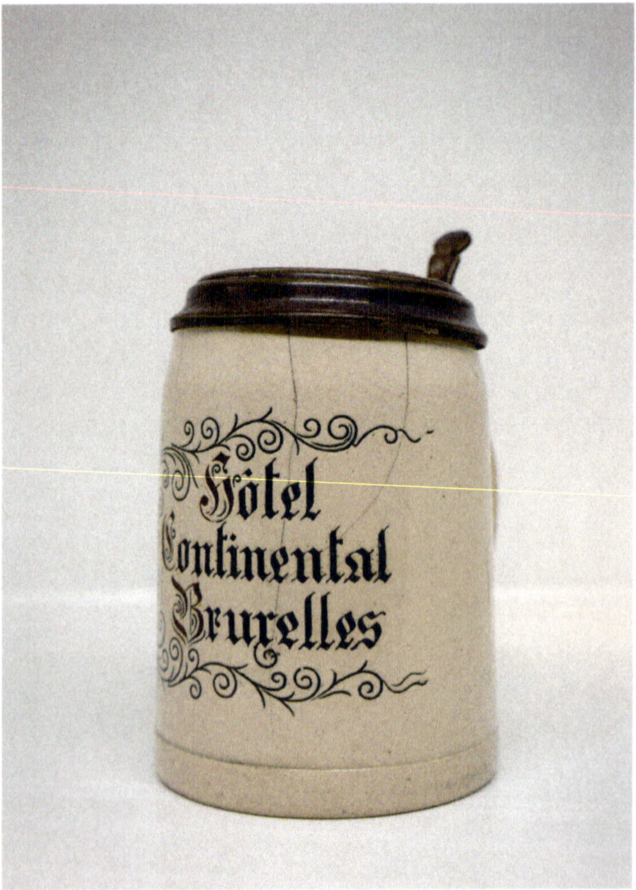
Hôtel
Continental
Bruxelles

#20
Hotel Continental Stein
1890s

- Pub Life

Brussels in 1895 was very different to the city overrun by revolutionary French troops a century earlier. The French were eventually kicked out, as were the Dutch royals that followed. Brussels became the capital of a new, independent Belgium, and by the late-19th century, it showed. Broad Haussmanian boulevards replaced the Zenne in the centre of the city, its economic importance having long since been usurped by the Brussels-Charleroi canal. Linking Brussels to Wallonian coal country, the canal helped turbocharge Brussels' industrialisation, spawning a *petit Manchester* and an affluent middle class. This was a bourgeoisie scornful of traditional Brussels estaminets. Instead, they wanted a place to show off their new-found prosperity. Somewhere like the Parisian café.

Brussels was a café latecomer, its first - the *Milles Colonnes* - opened in 1825. 60 years later however, as an article in *Le Globe Illustré* magazine declaimed, clamour for a new drinking experience was undeniable: "The old places no longer suffice. We want bigger establishments, we are not satisfied any more with Faro and Lambic, we demand hops." A place where *Bruxellois* were served by a tuxedoed waiter in gaslit rooms stuffed with doric columns, ornate woodwork, palm fronds and ferns. Where the walls were decorated with mirrors, and large windows provided a view onto the streets outside. Where a man could drink from his stein while his female companion nursed a glass of Amontillado. Where French literary exiles nursed their grudges and Belgian politicians staged pitched battles over doctrinal minutiae. Where an evening might start with a game of chess at the *Milles Colonnes*, before billiards and checkers at *Café des Trois Suisses*.

The names of these new cafés revealed their cosmopolitan ambitions. The *Grande Taverne Anglaise. Café de l'Europe. L'Hôtel-Café Continental*. Built in 1874 on a wedge of land where the new central boulevards bifurcated, the Continental's awning-covered terrace looked out onto a new city square. Home for a time to a wax museum, like many cafés it hosted a lively assortment of clubs and societies, hosting meetings of the *Véloce club Bruxellois*, an artists' circle, and the rowdy gatherings of Belgium's liberal party. The Continental was eventually joined on the square, christened Place De Brouckère in 1893, by a rival café run by an ambitious brewing family. Hounded out of central Brussels by the public works to bury the Zenne river in the 1870s, the Wielemans soon returned as café landlords. Their crowning achievement was the Café Metropole, opened in 1890 and expanded in 1894 to the Hôtel Metropole - the grandest of Brussels' *grands boulevards* hotels.

A catastrophic fire in 1901 gutted the Continental. But rebuilt in 1910, it helped make Place De Brouckère the epicentre of *fin de siècle* Brussels nightlife. Folklorist Louis Quiévreux called the square's cacophonous attractions - cafés, cinemas, theatres - "*Timesquaresque*". Jacques Brel immortalised it in his song *Bruxelles* as a place where men in collapsible top hats and women in crinoline watched the omnibus pass by through the windows of a café, and a time when Brussels "*bruxelait*".

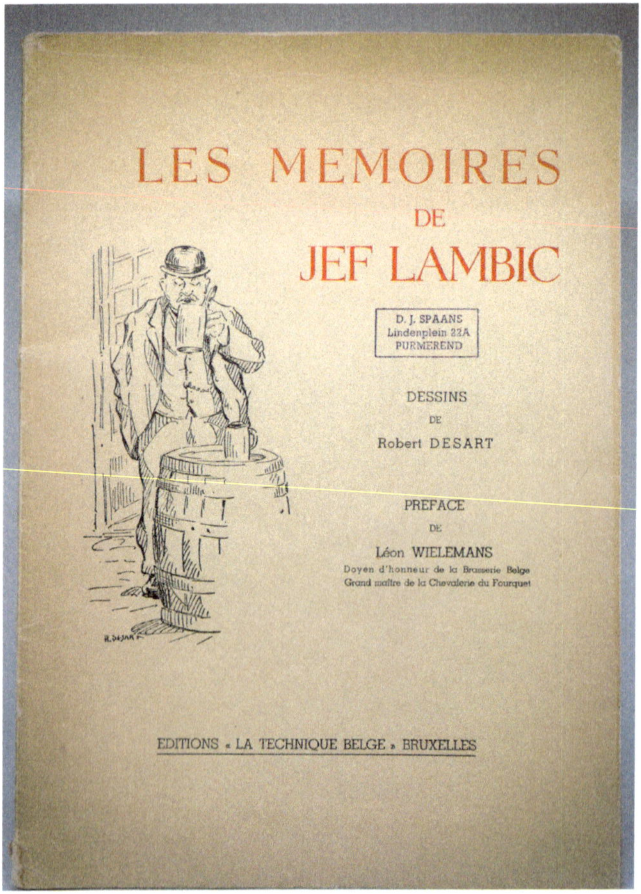
LES MEMOIRES
DE
JEF LAMBIC
D. J. SPAANS
Lindenplein 22A
PURMEREND
DESSINS
DE
Robert DESART
PREFACE
DE
Léon WIELEMANS
Doyen d'honneur de la Brasserie Belge
Grand maître de la Chevalerie du Fourquet
EDITIONS « LA TECHNIQUE BELGE » BRUXELLES

#21

Les Mémoires de Jef Lambic
1860/1958

- City Life

By the late 1800s, a new kind of café emerged in Brussels: the *café du coin* or *volkscafé*, a synthesis of the pre-industrial estaminet's proletarian atmosphere with the modernity - gaslight, mirrors, and foreign beers - of the city's bourgeois boulevard cafés. Part working man's club, part safe-deposit box, and part working class community centre, volkscafés became as intrinsic a part of Brussels' urban fabric as Amsterdam's bruine cafés or backstreet London boozers.

Many volkscafés have since vanished or evolved into something different, but we know so much about the vibrancy of their *fin de siècle* heyday because of one man's memoirs. A brewer's son, Jef Lambic was born in Brussels' working class Marollen neighbourhood in 1860 and grew up "between good-smelling wooden barrels and...cool cellars [with] a pleasant, slightly sour odor." His 20s coincided with Brussels' café boom, and Jef dived right in.

He experienced first hand the "brown beer invasion", the arrival of English beer, and Brussels' Bavarian Lager craze. Jef was *Zelig*-like, as comfortable conversing with the thick-necked café bosses of the Vlaamsesteenweg as he was ordering choucroute and a two litres of Löwenbrau from M. Kartoffel at the glittering Café des Trois Suisses.

Jef, however, always remained loyal to his "marvellous Brussels beer". His preference was Faro and Lambic in cellar bars on the Grand Place or in basements like those of the Hopital Saint Pierre, redolent of malt and hops rather than medicine. In *Mémoires d'un Pottezuyper* (Brussels dialect for drunk), written in his late-80s, Jef says he consumed two litres of Lambic, one of Faro and two more of table beer daily - 70,000 litres of Lambic across his lifetime.

In *Les Mémoires*, published posthumously in 1958, Jef is adept at colourful character sketches of café regulars. There is the aforementioned Kartoffel, German and obsessed with statistics. Mie Tête, Brussels' most beautiful and largest barmaid, with whom Jef fell madly in love. Or the *kwaksalver*, a drunken, "despicable pest". And then Jef himself, in bowler hat, wool-lined overcoat and pencil moustache, toasting the café *baes*.

Only, neither Jef nor his moustache ever existed. His memoirs are a fabrication, a *zwanze*, and the evidence is in the book. His birthday is April 1. His surname's ridiculous nominative determinism. And the manner of the book's "discovery" after Jef's "death" in the early 1950s - found, carefully wrapped and intact, in an abandoned beer barrel unearthed during construction work in the Marollen.

So who wrote Jef's memoirs? The Lambic.info website suggests the book's true author was its illustrator,

Robert Desart. Writer Roel Mulder points to other, alternative Brussels-based ghost writers. Shortly after the book's publication in 1958, a review in Le Soir confidently credited it to Desart. But does it matter that Jef's life is a fiction? As the Le Soir article says, "[Jef] revitalises the taverns of old, their mustached bosses, [and] their buxom waitresses ....sure, there are some inaccuracies ....but they in no way affect the evocation of this era, which remains utterly authentic."

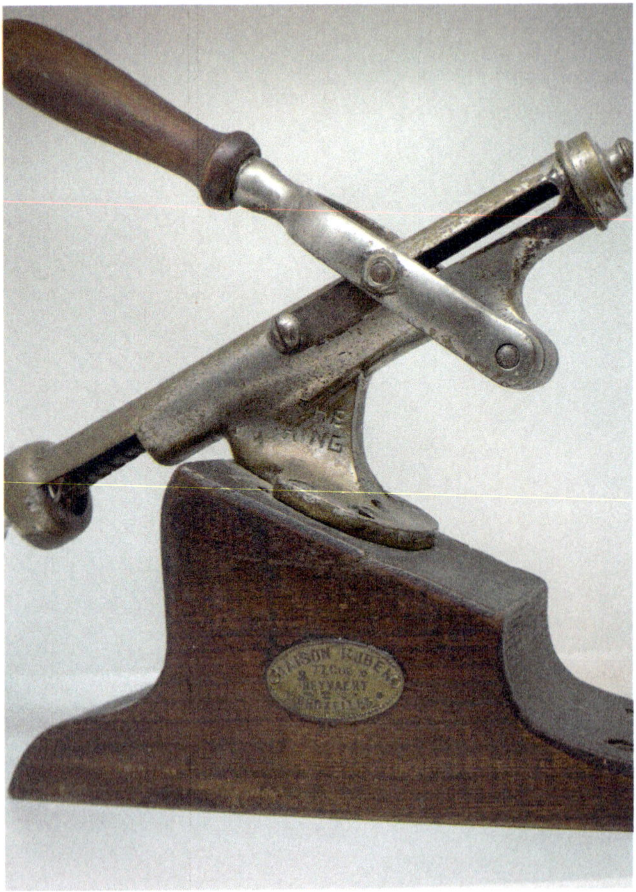

#22

Tire-Bouchon

1890s

- Pub Life

By the late 1800s, traditional Belgian brewing needed a lifeline. Their country had never had as many breweries or cafés, but it was Bavarian Bock beer not Belgian *bières brunes* these new brewers were making and cafés were serving.

How could these traditional brewers compete with foreign beers offering a clarity, effervescence and crispness that had thus far eluded them? The new *Spéciale Belge*, or Belgian Pale Ale, style made famous by Palm and De Koninck, was one answer. But brewers in Brussels came up with something different: *Gueuze*.

Well, not exactly. Before it became synonymous with a sparkling, bottled Lambic blend, "Gueuze" had long been in use as a term for unblended Lambic served flat from wooden barrels. In fact, many variations on the name - *Lambic des gueux, Lambic Gueuse, Geuzenlambic* - with one source suggesting it originated from French drinkers exclaiming *"cette gueuse de bière!"* ("That *wretch* of a beer!") after a few glasses.

As early as the 1850s *"Lambic et Lambic (gueuse)"* were sold side by side. Once Lambic brewers and blenders mastered the bottle conditioning of Lambic, Gueuze began to take its now-familiar form: a blend of variously-aged Lambic, conditioned in green champagne bottles, and corked. Once opened by a countertop metal *tire-bouchon* (corkscrew), this *Lambic Gueuze* was (relatively) clear, foamy, and highly carbonated.

Its big break came at the Brussels International Exposition in 1897, when over 9 months Expo visitors drank 4,405 litres of "Lambic-Gueuze", compared to 49,500 litres of Faro, 24,000 of Brune, 18,000 of Bock, 17,700 of Petit-Bavière, 8,000 of Munich and 12,417 litres of Lambic.

Gueuze's popularity continued to grow in the immediate pre-WWI years, but instead of outmaneuvering Bock beer it cannibalised its Brussels stablemates. Bad Lambic could always be rescued by a canny blender with a bit of sugar and post-production adulteration. But Gueuze had to be right from bottling.

And because blending a Gueuze required more precision than Lambic or Faro - requiring the right balance of young beer for carbonation and old beer for character - brewers and blenders tended to reserve their best Lambics for Gueuze production. The two beers were also competitively priced; for 10 centimes more, a drinker could get a foamy, sparkling Gueuze instead of a flat, turbid Lambic.

One brewer, Albert Vossen, writing in the 1950s, attributed Gueuze's success to another, less obvious benefit, proclaiming it "excellent, smooth, [and] easy on the digestion....a marvelous beer for weak people, fortifying and restorative…[and] an [excellent] beer for diabetics."

Health merits or otherwise of Gueuze aside, its supplanting of Lambic and Faro in the hearts and glasses of Brussels drinkers was inexorable. It accelerated after 1918 as consumer tastes shifted once more. Lambic was a 19th century beer, a hangover from Brussel's pre-industrial past. Gueuze, a product of its modern, industrialising future, was a beer for the 20th century. And on café shelves across the city, earthenware Lambic jugs eventually ceded their place to the *tires-bouchons* of the iron foundries.

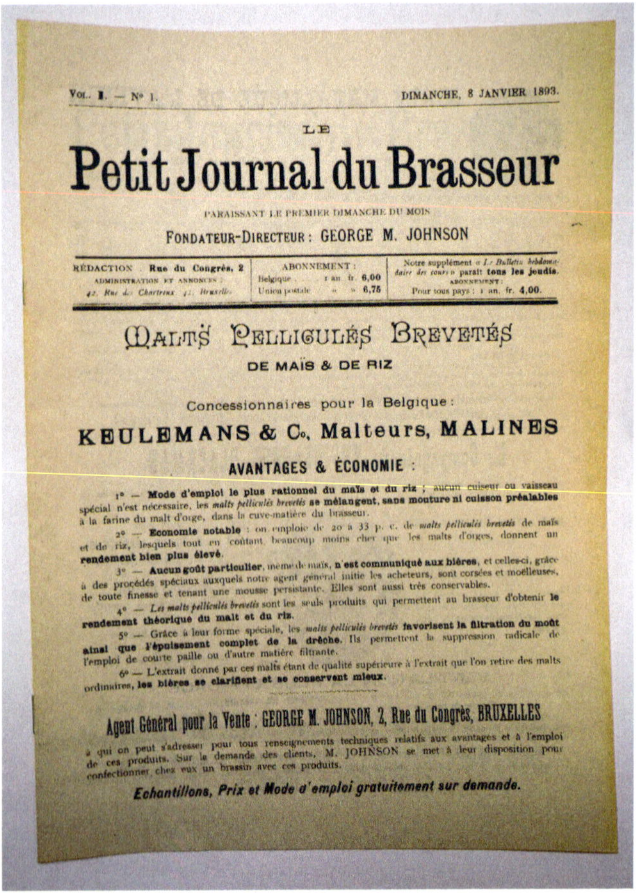

VOL. I. — N° 1. DIMANCHE, 8 JANVIER 1893.

LE

Petit Journal du Brasseur

PARAISSANT LE PREMIER DIMANCHE DU MOIS

FONDATEUR-DIRECTEUR : GEORGE M. JOHNSON

RÉDACTION : **Rue du Congrès, 2** ADMINISTRATION ET ANNONCES : *42, Rue des Chartreux, 42, Bruxelles*	ABONNEMENT : Belgique . . . 1 an. fr. **6,00** Union postale » » **6,75**	Notre supplément « *Le Bulletin hebdomadaire des cours* » paraît **tous les jeudis.** ABONNEMENT : Pour tous pays : 1 an. fr. **4,00.**

MALTS PELLICULÉS BREVETÉS

DE MAÏS & DE RIZ

Concessionnaires pour la Belgique :

KEULEMANS & Co, Malteurs, MALINES

AVANTAGES & ÉCONOMIE :

1° — **Mode d'emploi le plus rationnel du maïs et du riz** ; aucun cuiseur ou vaisseau spécial n'est nécessaire, les *malts pelliculés brevetés* **se mélangent, sans mouture ni cuisson préalables** à la farine du malt d'orge, dans la cuve-matière du brasseur.

2° — **Economie notable** : on emploie de 20 à 33 p. c. de *malts pelliculés brevetés* de maïs et de riz, lesquels tout en coûtant beaucoup moins cher que les malts d'orges, donnent un **rendement bien plus élevé**.

3° — **Aucun goût particulier**, même de maïs, **n'est communiqué aux bières**, et celles-ci, grâce à des procédés spéciaux auxquels notre agent général initie les acheteurs, sont corsées et moëlleuses, de toute finesse et tenant une mousse persistante. Elles sont aussi très conservables.

4° — *Les malts pelliculés brevetés* sont les seuls produits qui permettent au brasseur d'obtenir **le rendement théorique du malt et du riz**.

5° — Grâce à leur forme spéciale, les *malts pelliculés brevetés* **favorisent la filtration du moût ainsi que l'épuisement complet de la drêche.** Ils permettent la suppression radicale de l'emploi de courte paille ou d'autre matière filtrante.

6° — L'extrait donné par ces maltŝ étant de qualité supérieure à l'extrait que l'on retire des malts ordinaires, **les bières se clarifient et se conservent mieux**.

Agent Général pour la Vente : GEORGE M. JOHNSON, 2, Rue du Congrès, BRUXELLES

à qui on peut s'adresser pour tous renseignements techniques relatifs aux avantages et à l'emploi de ces produits. Sur la demande des clients, M. JOHNSON se met à leur disposition pour confectionner chez eux un brassin avec ces produits.

Echantillons, Prix et Mode d'emploi gratuitement sur demande.

#23

Le Petit Journal du Brasseur, № 1

1890s

- Business Life

Once upon time, a young brewer's son from Canterbury in England became the godfather of modern Belgian beer. It all started on Sunday, 8 January 1893, with the appearance of edition one of *Le Petit Journal du Brasseur*. Only 10 pages long, its cover featured an advert for patented corn and rice malts, below which someone called George M. Johnson was identified as being available to visit interested breweries for a product demonstration. George M. (for Maw) Johnson also happened to be the paper's Founder-Editor, having arrived in Brussels three years previously with a missionary zeal to bring Belgian brewing into the modern, industrial age.

George's family were originally jewellers, until his father (also George) bought the Northgate Brewery in Canterbury in 1866. George Maw - eldest of 17 children - worked with his father for three years before turning up at Brussels' Brasserie Leopold in 1890. It was auspicious timing; Belgian brewers considered England one of the world's most advanced brewing nations, far ahead of their own. As head of Leopold's laboratory,

Johnson failed at his first attempt at a brewer's journal. The *Petit Journal du Brasseur* was his second, a monthly publication released on Sundays that cost six francs annually. In his first editorial, he welcomed readers with the immodest expectation they would "greet with joy the new era of enlightenment and brewing progress which, without a doubt, will be born thanks to the....*Petit Journal*".

The *Petit Journal* was, Johnson said, "devoted to technical and industrial issues of interest to the brewery", and edition one established the paper's template. Articles on technical matters - edition one covered the aeration of hot and cold malts, chill haze affecting top fermented beers stored in cold cellars, and the issue of applying pitch and varnish internally or externally on wooden barrels - were joined by letters from brewers with technical questions and adverts for yeast suppliers, maltings, and surplus brewery stock.

There were also listings of the latest raw materials prices, Moldavian malt costing 21-23 francs/kilo in January 1893. Later editions would cover water's essential role in brewing, the potential impact of Irish Home Rule on British brewing (Johnson was anti-Home Rule), and the impact of changeable weather on Bavarian hop yields.

Johnson had found a financially successful formula, and with Belgium's breweries having few formally educated brewing engineers in the 1890s they came to rely on the *Petit Journal* for in-house technical support. In the next decade the *Petit Journal* shifted to a weekly schedule, absorbing a Belgian rival and their French counterpart.

Then, in 1914, publication stopped. Escaping war, George made it to England. Henri Codville, George's son-in-law and right-hand man ended up working in a munitions factory. Following armistice the pair returned to Brussels and a brewing industry transformed. In the immediate aftermath of WWI, brewers were less focused on expansion than on reconstruction, profitability, and efficiency. And they wanted to brew English beers. Something George Maw, returned to the *Petit Journal*'s editorial chair, knew a thing or two about.

Frantz Fonson
Fernand Wicheler

Le Mariage de Mlle Beulemans

théâtre

#24

Le Mariage de Mlle Beulemans

1910

- City Life

On March 18, 1910, theatregoers filed into the Théâtre de l'Olympia's auditorium for the premiere of a new play. The proscenium curtain lifted to reveal a man and woman, both young, sitting in an office. A sign hanging behind them said *Beulemans, seul dépositaire du stout Glascow* [sic] ("Beulemans, sole proprietor of Glasgow Stout").

The woman is Suzanne, the proprietor's daughter. She is discussing an order for Beulemans' Petit Bavière with Albert Delpierre, a Frenchman in Brussels to learn the beer trade but struggling to adapt, unable to curl his Parisian tongue around Brussels' dialect. Albert is also madly in love with Suzanne. Who is, unfortunately, engaged to Seraphin Meulemeester, a member of Brussels' society of brewers. Suzanne's father, Ferdinand Beulemans, covets the society's honorary president position.

Beulemans *père* enters the scene, to complain about Albert botching a delivery of 100 bottles of stout, exclaiming, "I'm the only supplier of 'Stout Glascow'....You can't mess that up!" And so begins *Le Mariage de Mlle*

Beulemans ("The Marriage of Ms. Beulemans").

"[A] great farce, [featuring] frequent vulgarity" said an early reviewer of *Beulemans*. The work of Fernand Wicheler and Frantz Fonson - respectively a journalist and the then-director of the Théâtre des Galeries - it was a gentle satire on *fin de siècle* Brussels. Fonson's father ran a military supply factory, and he grew up surrounded by characters from Brussels' commercial class. Beulemans could have been a textiles, paper, or ironmongery magnate, but that he was a brewer (or beer merchant, it's unclear) reflects the industry's establishment credentials.

There were roughly 100 breweries in Brussels in 1910 - small neighbourhood breweries, industrial behemoths, traditional Lambic producers, and Pilsner factories. Brewers hadn't regained their pre-Revolutionary political influence, but were by the 1900s a ubiquitous thread in the city's social fabric. *Beulemans* wears its brewing knowledge lightly; aside from mislaid beer shipments, Beulemans is most beer-centric in the third act, when the society of brewers host their annual meeting in a estaminet backroom and Albert defends Beulemans as a "man of the people" who has fought against foreign imports and in defence of Belgian beer standards.

And by the play's end, Beulemans, with Albert's help, has secured his honorary title, Suzanne has left her fiance for Albert, and the Beulemans family are serenaded at the estaminet by the city's brewers cheering the name "Beulemans!" on the street outside.

Beulemans was an immediate success. It ran uninterrupted until May, ending 1910 with over 300 performances across Brussels and Paris. Local audiences in particular took corpulent, vain Beulemans to their hearts because, a contemporary review said, he remained an earthy *Bruxellois* even as he became a successful brewer, and Brussels' theatregoers appreciated the "faithful mirror" it held up to the language and mannerisms of the city's residents.

But its popularity transcended Brussels, with productions in Italy, Algeria, and in Buenos Aires - often with tweaks to the format for local consumption. English playwrights, for example, recast Beulemans as Enos Lllewelyn, a Carmarthen-based wineseller with a monopoly concession on Champagne.

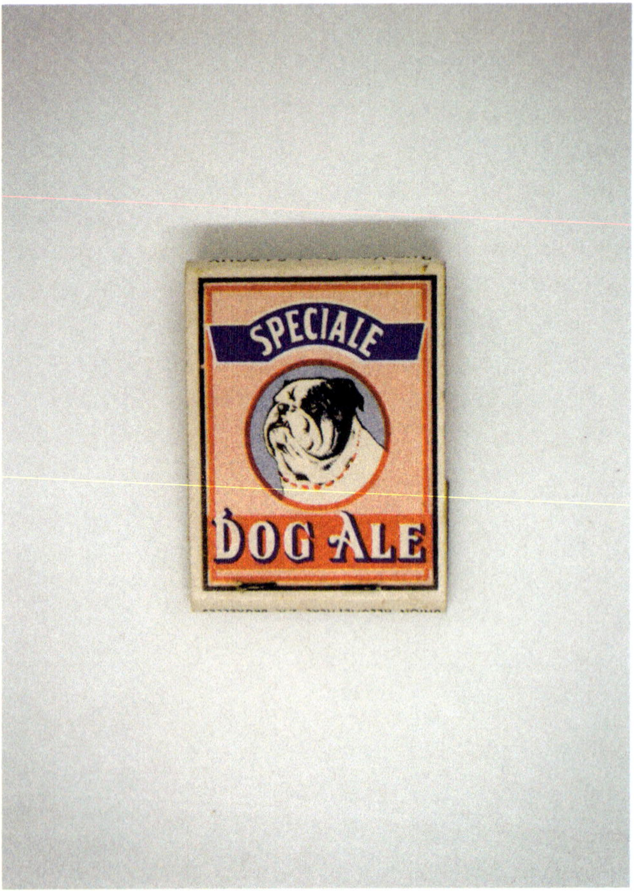
SPECIALE
DOG ALE

#25
Dog Ale Matchbox
1920s

- Brewery Life

In post-1918 Brussels, German beer was out and English beer was in. That may be an oversimplification of the city's beer industry in the years immediately following WWI. Breweries in Brussels did continue to make Bavarian Lager beers throughout the 1920s. And English beer's presence in the city long-predated post-war Anglomania. London's Whitbread brewery for example established their own bottling and distribution centre in Molenbeek in 1907, and in 1913 Belgium imported 154,037 hectolitres of Pale Ales, Stouts and Scotch Ales.

Following the Germans withdrawal in November 1918, English beer's popularity resumed its upward trajectory. On Christmas Day 1919 the Royal Greenwich café at the Botanique was advertising "the celebrated beers Pale Ale, Stout Worthington, as well as the Scotch Ale [and] Christmas Ale Mac-Ewan [sic])". Trade magazines and newspapers were full of colourful advertisements for Bass Pale-Ale and Stout alongside Campbell and Co.'s Royal Edinburgh Christmas Beer, and by 1920 annual English beer imports reached 159,750 hectolitres.

Then, all of a sudden, imports plummeted. One

brewery claimed to be behind their precipitous decline: Brasserie Wielemans-Ceuppens in Vorst. Having moved from brewing traditional Lambic and Faro to Munich and Petit Bavière in the 1880s, by 1927 the Wielemans brothers were proclaiming their Crown Trees Stout and Scotch as "vanquishers of the foreigners" that were almost single-handedly responsible for reducing annual English beer imports to a paltry 71,000 hectolitres. Wielemans offered what Brussels' drinkers wanted - English beer - but at a more competitive price point and delivered through its extensive network of Brussels cafés.

Brewing in Brussels had suffered grievously during the war. But by the early 1920s production capacity in the capital was recovering, and Wielemans were not alone in seeking the lucrative market share of the Pale Ales and Stouts of their English rivals. Brasserie du Marly, on the canal in Neder-over-Heembeek, found success with Navy's Scotch Ale, Bark Ale and Sweet Stout. In Molenbeek the Vandenheuvel brewery brewed a Stout V.D.B. and Christmas Holly Stout.

Schaarbeek's Brasserie Roelants (or Roelandts), founded around 1900 and located near the railway sidings in the Collignon neighbourhood, also hitched their post-war recovery to the English bandwagon. Roelants produced a diverse range of beers - alongside Faro, Bock and Munich, they brewed a Scotch and Big Ben Stout, made "according [to] English process" according to the beer's label. But perhaps their most popular, or at least most advertised, English-style beer was their Speciale Dog Ale.

Lacking the industrial scale of the Wielemans, Roelants pitched themselves as a David among goliaths. Dog Ale was their slingshot, the "perfect imitation of the English Pale Ale", brewed by Roelants "[t]o English tastes but Belgium-made and sold at Belgian prices". Contemporary advertisements claimed the beer would make English-brewed Pale Ale drinkers jealous of Dog Ale drinkers, who in turn would become condescendingly sympathetic towards these rubes for not choosing a Roelants. And ever-present in the ad copy the Dog Ale drinker was accompanied by the Englishman's best friend, the loyal British bulldog.

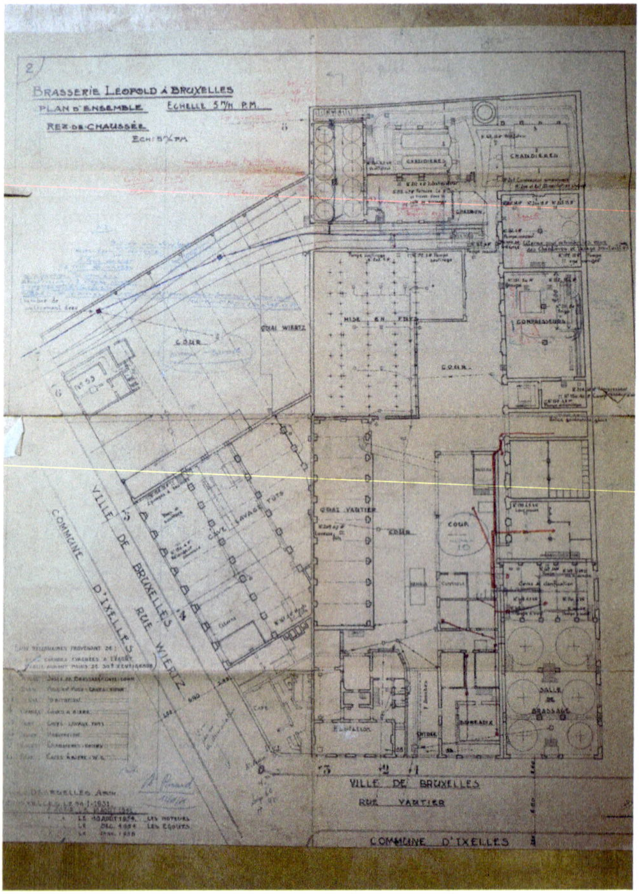
BRASSERIE LEOPOLD À BRUXELLES
PLAN D'ENSEMBLE
REZ-DE-CHAUSSÉE
CHAUDIERES
MISE EN FUTS
QUAI WIERTZ
COUR
COMPRESSEURS
QUAI VANTIER
CAVE LAVAGE FUTS
VILLE DE BRUXELLES
RUE WIERTZ
COMMUNE D'IXELLES
SALLE DE BRASSAGE
VILLE DE BRUXELLES
RUE VANTIER
COMMUNE D'IXELLES

#26

Plan for Brasserie Léopold

1931

- Brewery Life

Brussels in the 1920s was hit hard by a virulent case of Anglophilia, with cafés and estaminets overflowing with Stouts, Pale Ales, and Scotch. But the locally-brewed, Bavarian-inspired beers that had dominated brewing in Brussels before 1914 didn't disappear altogether. Breweries continued to make Munichs and Bocks alongside their English equivalents, and advertisements like those of the Grandes Brasseries d'Ixelles - touting an eclectic range featuring an Export Helles, King's Stout, Super Munich, and Gold Pearl Scotch - were commonplace.

It was a financially lucrative formula, ushering in an interbellum golden age for Brussels brewing which in turn launched an unprecedented building boom in the late 1920s and early 1930s. Wielemans-Ceuppens in Vorst commissioned a blocky modernist brewery from renowned architect Adrien Blomme, reputedly the largest in Europe when completed. Brasserie St Michel (later Vandenheuvel) expanded their footprint next to the Brussels West station in Molenbeek. And Anderlecht's Grandes Brasseries Atlas erected a 30m-tall Moderne-style brewery tower.

Brasserie Léopold wasn't as large as some of their rivals; in 1922, for example, the brewery consumed 1.6 million kilos of grain compared to Wielemans' six million. But the Damiens family who ran Léopold were ambitious. Founded in 1860 - on a plot now occupied by the European Parliament - and sharing its name both with the next-door train station and the neighbourhood in which it was located, Léopold originally focused on producing Lambic and Faro. By the 1920s they too had started brewing foreign beer styles as the brewery's director Georges Damiens was determined to not be left behind by his rivals elsewhere in Brussels.

If Léopold were to properly compete, though, Damiens decided they would need to expand. The existing brewery complex was adapted based on plans by local architect Alex Desruelles. It featured a home for Damiens, an on-site café, cellars for the brewery's 22-tonne square open fermentation vessels capable of holding 223 hectolitres of beer, and three floors built for its 38-tonne, 325-hectolitre lagering tanks. A new brewery required new equipment - brewing vessels, piping, engines - to make the beers Damiens wanted. For this, local expertise was insufficient. Instead, Léopold's director looked east, to the Stuttgart suburb of Feuerbach.

Feuerbach was home to the *A. Ziemann Maschinenfabrik für Brauereienlagen*. Ziemann were a well-established engineering firm that had built one of the first industrial breweries in China (Tsingtao brewery), as well as supplying Berlin brewery Berliner-Kindl with their equipment and - closer to home - had worked with Wielemans-Ceuppens before the war.

In June 1930 Ziemann drafted plans for a new six-kettle, steam-powered *Sudhaus* ("brewery") for Brasserie Léopold capable of brewing 92 *Zentner* (4600 kg) of malt per batch. It included *Laüterbottichen* (lauter tuns), *Maischbottichpfannen* (mash boilers), and a *Hopfenmontejus* (a hop-back), which Ziemann's engineers recommended to avoid the leaching of "unfavourable bitter resins" from hop cones into Léopold's beer.

Construction and delivery would take Ziemann eight months and installation on-site in Brussels a further six. And the damage this would cause to Damiens' and Léopold's finances? The princely sum of 18,168 Reichsmarks (€63,360).

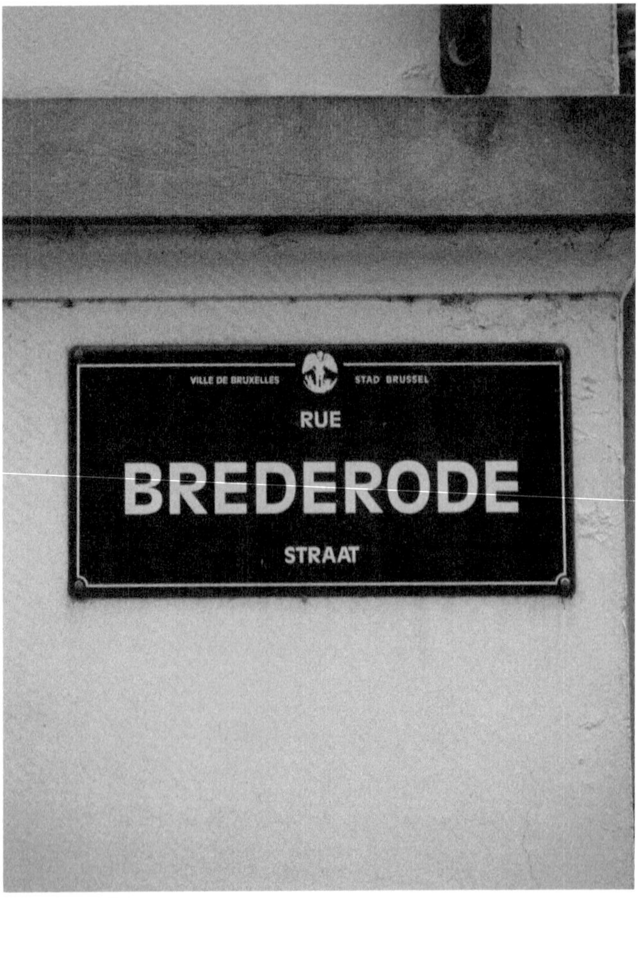
VILLE DE BRUXELLES
STAD BRUSSEL
RUE
BREDERODE
STRAAT

#27
Rue Brederode
1920s-1950s

- Business Life

Brussels' interwar brewing boom didn't restrict itself to the Belgian capital's borders. Potential investors also looked further afield, to Belgium's central African colonies.

The Belgian state took control of the Congo in 1908, following the exposure by Roger Casement of the pervasive brutality and human rights violations of King Leopold II's privately-owned Congo Free State. The Belgian state imposed an extractive colonial economy on the region. By the early 1920s the financial backers of Belgian colonialism began investing heavily in industrial development, to circumvent the cost of shipping goods from Europe and to undercut imports from colonial rivals.

Brasseries Katanga in Elisabethville (now Lubumbashi), was established in 1923 by the eponymous region's wealthy mining companies to replace the German beer mine workers had been drinking with a locally-made, Belgian-owned alternative. In October of the same year *Brasserie de Léopoldville* was founded in the capital Léopoldville (now Kinshasa), and by 1927 the Léopoldville brewery was selling 815,500 beers, with Primus as its flagship brand.

But the profits of these sales of Primus didn't stay in Léopoldville, instead being siphoned back to Belgium to its main shareholder, Brussels' *Banque de Bruxelles*. Similarly, *Brasseries Katanga* was backed by the *Compagnie du Congo pour le Commerce et l'Industrie (CCCI)*, the colonial investment arm of the *Société Générale de Belgique*. The *Société Générale* was Belgian colonialism's "great vampire squid", whose avaricious tentacles held the Congolese economy in an asphyxiating grip, controlling the market in diamonds, copper, radium - and beer.

Brewing was a successful investment. In 1952 Brasseries Katanga were paying out 562m Francs in dividends. Most of this money would have made its way back to the CCCI's headquarters at 13, Rue Brederode. Taking up almost an entire block, it stood at a nexus of Belgian colonial capitalism. Nearby buildings housed the *Banque d'Outremer*, a significant colonial investment vehicle, the *Banque du Congo Belge*, and the *Banque Belge d'Afrique*. Across the street was the *Chalet Suisse*, which previously housed the administration of Leopold's Congo Free State, and behind the chalet was Brussels' royal palace. A short walk downhill was the Ministry of Colonial Affairs, and further along *Société Générale*'s headquarters.

In the 1950s another *Société Générale*-backed brewery (with investment from Belgium's Brouwerij Haacht) from Stanleyville (now Kisangani) sought to challenge Primus' dominance of Léopoldville. Brasseries du

Congo, or Bracongo, were known for the slender green bottles of their Polar brand. In September 1957 Bracongo hired a former postal worker, recently-released from prison following an embezzlement conviction, to help sell them. Patrice Lumumba not only grew Polar's business in the capital, he also used his salesman skills and his client network to advocate for Congolese independence.

When Lumumba quit Bracongo in 1958 to focus on politics, his former customers became locations for meetings and rallies where attendees would ask not for a Polar but "'Pesa ngai Lumumba' ('Give me a Lumumba')." Two years later, the former beer salesman found himself in Brussels, a stone's throw from Rue Brederode in Leopold's royal palace, demanding Congolese independence.

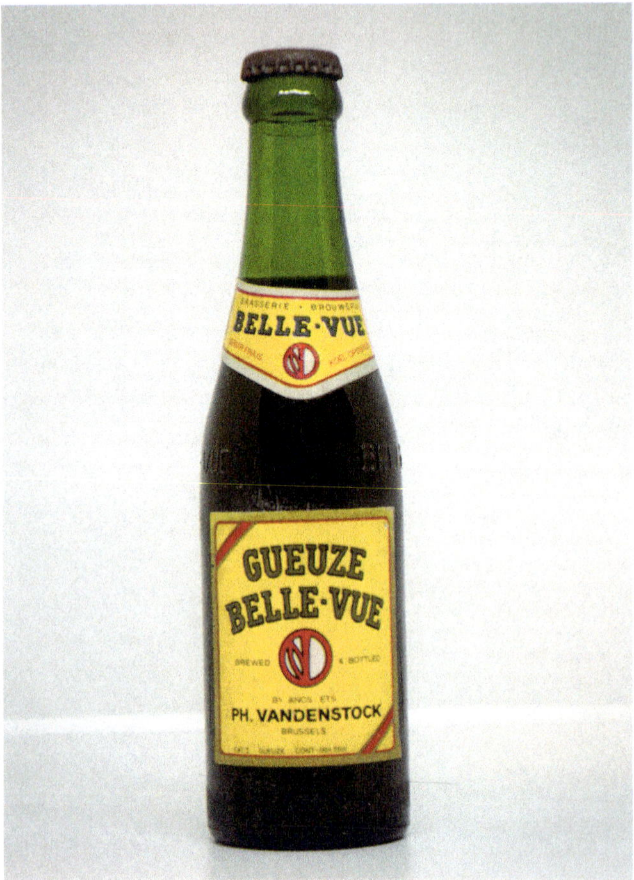
GUEUZE
BELLE·VUE
BREWED
& BOTTLED
PH. VANDENSTOCK
BRUSSELS

#28

Gueuze Belle-Vue

1950s

- Brewery Life

How quickly can one beer obliterate centuries of brewing tradition? Very, if the fate of Brussels' Lambic brewers is any measure. The privations of a second German occupation in 30 years - equipment requisitioned, scarce raw materials, and the enforced brewing of low-ABV *fluitjesbier* - meant the city's breweries emerged vulnerable from WWII. Lambic brewers shared a particular vulnerability their conventional counterparts did not, a weakness most of them couldn't escape.

Lambic, because of its archaic production methods, is more vulnerable than most beers to environmental fluctuations. Hot summers can spoil Lambic as it ferments in wooden barrels, by encouraging the propagation of unwanted microbes and unwanted flavours. And once this Lambic has been blended and bottled as a Gueuze, hot summers can cause these bottles to spontaneously pop their corks and even explode.

Which is exactly what happened in the summer of 1949. The temperature reached 36 degrees in parts of Belgium, and in Brussels three million bottles exploded in the cellars and storerooms of the city's Lambic breweries. There was one brewery that escaped the heatwave largely unscathed. And Brasserie Belle-Vue managed this because their Gueuze was not like the others.

Belle-Vue began life as a café, where Josef-Philemon Vanden Stock blended Lambic behind the bar. In 1943 Vanden Stock bought the defunct VosKina brewery in nearby Molenbeek, putting his son Constant to work. When Josef-Philemon was deported by the Germans to a concentration camp in August 1944, where he died less than a year later, Constant took on the job of guiding the family business through the wartime predations. He had a simple idea: make Gueuze more palatable. "Even as a child, I remarked that some people found Gueuze too hard," Constant said later. So he "made it a bit softer and rounder" by blending greater amounts of younger (sweeter) Lambic for Gueuze Belle-Vue. This more sugary Lambic required pasteurisation to prevent overactive bottle conditioning and with it potentially explosive consequences.

It was this pasteurisation that insulated Gueuze Belle-Vue from the extreme temperature fluctuations blowing up its rivals. And the divergences from Lambic orthodoxy kept coming. Gueuze Belle-Vue was filtered, to remove yeast sediment, artificially carbonated, and topped with a cap instead of a cork. It was served not in traditional, large champagne-style bottles but in dinky 250ml ones that sold better as single servings in cafés.

Belle-Vue's *Capsulekes Geuze* was tapping into a postwar consumer palate that was abandoning the tart complexity represented by traditional Lambic in favour of sweetness and simplicity. It was riotously successful, and rival Lambic producers could only keep up by imitating Belle-Vue's transgressions. Many tried, though others were unwilling or incapable of adapting to the post-war industrialisation, modernisation, and commodification of food production.

Fuelled by the success of Gueuze Belle-Vue (and the brewery's Kriek), the brewery hoovered up its beleaguered local rivals and relocated in 1969 to a new home on the canal.

In 25 short years Belle-Vue had become Brussels' pre-eminent Lambic brewery, and its weatherproof Gueuze had demolished a 200-year-old brewing tradition.

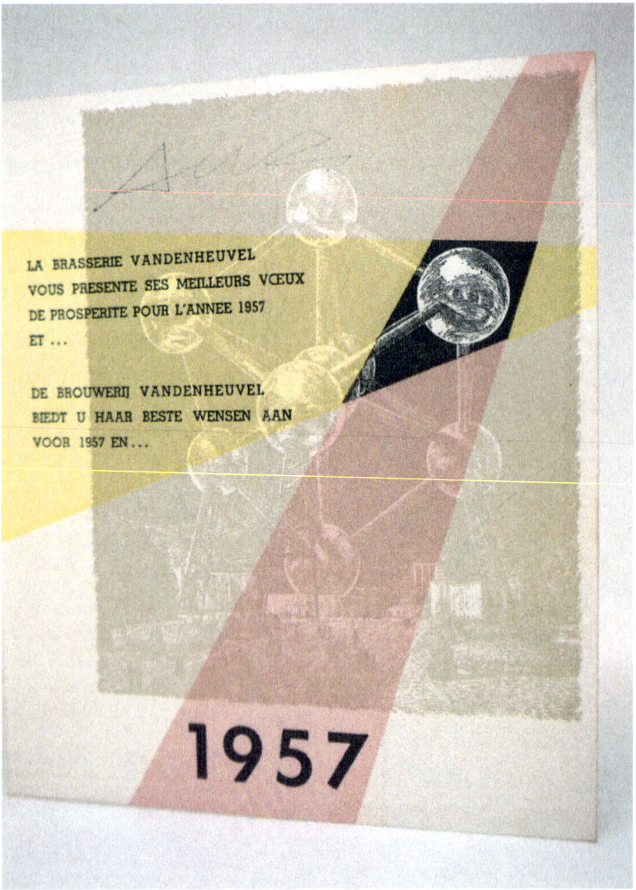
LA BRASSERIE VANDENHEUVEL
VOUS PRESENTE SES MEILLEURS VŒUX
DE PROSPERITE POUR L'ANNEE 1957
ET ...
DE BROUWERIJ VANDENHEUVEL
BIEDT U HAAR BESTE WENSEN AAN
VOOR 1957 EN...
1957

#29

Vandenheuvel New Year's Card

1957

- City Life

"Brasserie Vandenheuvel sends you its best wishes for 1957, and from now on is preparing to receive you with dignity at the World Exhibition Brussels 1958, where it will be represented in the Atomium, the main attraction of the Exhibition."

With these words Molenbeek's Vandenheuvel brewery said goodbye to 1957 and looked to a momentous year ahead. In 1958 Belgium invited the world to Brussels, across 200 hectares and 44 country pavilions, under the motto "a world for a better life for mankind". America brought the colour television, and Russia Sputnik (which mysteriously disappeared), but Expo '58 was above all about Belgium.

A new Belgium, emerging from post-war recovery as a proudly techno-optimistic country that was still (just about) a colonial power, with a young king, and not yet unravelled by bubbling communitarian division. Its symbol, and that of the Expo, was the Atomium, a temporary 102 metre-tall, nine-steel-ball edifice. When it opened in April 1958 the structure's bar served, as Vandenheuvel promised, the brewery's Ekla Pils.

Visitors unmoved by Ekla didn't lack for exotic alternatives. At the Atomium's base was the DAB Terrasse, offering krugs of Dortmunder Export. Löwenbräu erected the *Oberbayern* Bavarian *bierhalle* replete with roaring golden lion and blue-and-white bunting. Restaurant Praha had white-coated bartenders dispensing Pilsner Urquell paired with *bramboràk*. The British pavilion had Whitbread Pale Ale at the yacht club-themed Britannia or Jubilee Stout and John Smith's at the Fox and Hounds. There was Guinness at the American pavilion and the *Heinekens Hoek* at the Dutch. The Congolese section had Café Matadi, serving beers from the Léopold and Katanga breweries not far from a grizzly "human zoo".

Vandenheuvel and its Belgian contemporaries would not be outdone by these foreign interlopers. But in a deliberate act of counterprogramming, they eschewed steel and glass in favour of a Potemkin village of lanes and squares populated by replicas and pastiches of the country's historic architecture. The *Societe Cooperative "Belgique 1900"* in which all the major Brussels breweries participated - Wielemans, Roelants, Koekelberg (now Ixelberg), Léopold, and Vandenheuvel - financed this *Belgique Joyeuse* village, the point of which was that "...next to the futuristic metropolis of the Heizel...where the Atomium reigns [in] a universe of Leviathans, there would be a city of our childhoods, a village which could be called Lier, Diksmuide or Bastogne."

Buildings from Lier, Diksmuide or Bastogne featured, as did Antwerp (the Maison Plantin), Namur (the

Maison des Bouchers), Brussels (the Maison de Bellone), and beyond. 40 of them housed cafés, of which Vandenheuvel was responsible for seven, including a replica of the Cheval Marin restaurant on Brussels' Varkensmarkt.

When *Belgique Joyeuse* closed in October 1958, 4.5 million visitors had passed through its neo-renaissance fever dream, and many frothy glasses of Ekla were consumed in the Cheval Marin, the Willem Tell, or the Café Uylenspiegel. Writing their New Year's card for 1959, Vandenheuvel's owners must have been tempted to celebrate their business acumen and look optimistically towards what must have appeared like a prosperous decade ahead.

A History of Brussels Beer in 50 Objects

#30
«Curiosités et Anecdotes: La Gueuze»
1962

- Brewery Life

If Constant Vanden Stock was the future, by 1962 Albert Vossen was the past. Waiting to be interviewed by TV journalist Sélim Sasson for "Curiosités et anecdotes : la gueuze", Vossen must surely have known this.

Albert Vossen was a second-generation brewery owner, his father Theophile having started Brasserie Vossen on Brussels' Rue des Capucins in the early 1900s. Despite its name Vossens didn't brew, instead sourcing Lambic from other breweries, including the De Keersmaeker brewery in nearby Kobbegem. In 1927 Théophile bought the Mort Subite café, which subsequently lent its name to Vossen's Gueuze.

By the time *Radio-Télévision Belge* broadcast his interview, Albert had been fighting a long rearguard action in defence of traditional Lambic. In 1954 he'd given a lecture that, while ostensibly about similarities between Champagne and Gueuze, was ultimately a plea for the protection of Lambic culture against industrialisation. Albert lamented how "deeply sad and regrettable" it was that price wars and a decline in the quality of Lambic meant producers were "disregard[ing]...

the personality of the Gueuze of our fathers." By 1959 Albert had closed Brasserie Vossen, handing over its 3,000 Lambic-filled *pijpen* (old Porto barrels) to the *Union des Marchands des Bières*, a Lambic blenders' cooperative of which he was the secretary.

It was in this role that he appeared on Belgian television avuncularly explaining Lambic. But everything about the four-minute segment confirms the Vossens' world as one passing into folklore. The clip's title - "curiosities and anecdotes" - suggests traditional Lambic was already a relic of a bygone era rather than the staple beer of Brussels' estaminets and cafés it had been for almost two centuries. The footage - a dusty barrel-filled cellar populated by cloth-capped men wearing aprons, pencil moustaches and cravates - evokes a cottage industry aesthetic rather than a thriving contemporary business.

Then there's the interviewer's attitude. Sasson says he's looking for "historical truth", pitching questions about Lambic's nausea-inducing properties and if it's just a beer for the "common man". Vossen, all jowly smirk, twinkling eyes and expressive eyebrows, jovially disabuses Sasson of his muddled thinking: "It's a beer that gives joy! A beer that makes you sing, *monsieur*!" But there is, in his animated defence of Lambic, a sense that perhaps Vossen knows his world is slipping away.

Mid-way through the interview, talking about Lambic's long fermentation, Vossen says of his tribe: "We are fatalists". Fatalism was an understandable emotion for Lambic brewers in '60s and '70s Brussels. Those not bought out by a bigger rival went through the motions as production slowed, their Lambic vinegared in barrels, and their breweries eventually closed. In 1970, the Mort Subite café and brand was sold to the De Keermsakers, though the Vossen name remains above the bar's entrance. Albert Vossen died in 1978, the same year a young Lambic brewer in Anderlecht rejected the fatalism of his peers. Jean-Pierre Van Roy was determined to save the brewery he'd taken over from his father-in-law - even if it meant turning Brasserie Cantillon into a working museum.

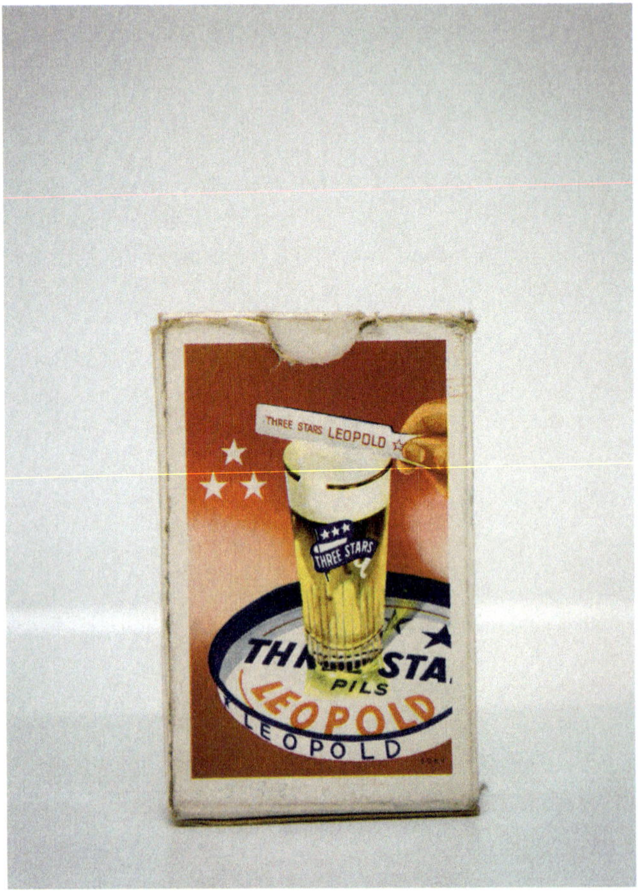
THREE STARS LEOPOLD
THREE STARS
PILS
LEOPOLD
LEOPOLD

#31

Three Stars Pils Playing Cards

1960s

- Pub Life

Brasserie Vandenheuvel's Ekla Pils was the belle of the Expo '58 ball, but it wasn't the only star of the show. At the *Belgique Joyeuse* village, drinkers could avail of Ixelberg's Elberg Pils, Jager-Pils from Schaarbeek's Brasserie Roelants, and Wiel's Pils from Wielemans-Ceuppens. At the exposition's futuristic Heliport - where VIPs were flown in by helicopter - Brasserie Léopold tapped their Three Stars Pils.

The Expo may have been temporary, but the move by Brussels' industrial breweries towards Pils in the late '50s and early '60s was permanent. For Brasserie Léopold, building on their rapid pre-WWII expansion and investment from Heineken, this meant ditching darker, sweeter Bock beers in favour of their lighter cousins - beers with pseudo-nautical names like White Star and Three Stars Pils.

Brewers were happy to brew these beers at scale, and Belgians were happy to drink them. As breweries expanded and streamlined production, and beer became increasingly commodified, industrial Pils brewing became Brussels' dominant business model. And, for a while, it was a successful formula. In the '60s and '70s Wielemans was regularly producing 500,000 hectolitres of beer annually. Vandenheuvel could fill 42,000 bottles an hour. And Léopold went on a minor buying spree, hoovering up smaller breweries in Overijse and Bruges. In 1969, at the peak of Pils mania, the ribbon-cutting ceremony for the central Brussels Danish Tavern - serving Tuborg and Carlsberg - was attended by King Baudouin and Queen Fabiola of Belgium, and Henrik, Prince Consort of Denmark.

Everything may have appeared placid on the surface, but the city's breweries were pedalling furiously to remain competitive. In a situation where everyone was brewing variations on the same theme, it often mattered less what was in the glass than it did which brewery could spend more (and better) on marketing and advertising - glassware, enamel bar signs, ashtrays, and decks of cards. Growth came increasingly from takeovers and consolidation, with smaller breweries being picked off by their deeper-pocketed rivals. Grande Brasserie de Koekelberg, which had already merged with the Ixelles brewery in the 1950s to form Ixelberg, bought Roelants in 1962, and were themselves swallowed up by Vandenheuvel in 1969.

As Léopold, Wielemans, and Vandenheuvel struggled to emerge as Brussels' dominant Pils-brewing force, outside rivals regarded the city's market with envious eyes, slowly and surely drawing their plans against it. Vandenheuvel was bought by English brewery Watneys and closed in 1974. Léopold staggered on, until the economic shocks of the early 1970s forced its Dutch investor to sell to Artois of Leuven in 1976. Sales of Three Star Pils in keg remained robust, but Artois' purchase agreement prevented Léopold from selling bottled beer to the large drinks warehouses that supply Belgium's cafés.

The brewery staggered on until 1981, when Artois finally pulled the plug. In barely two decades, Pils had come to utterly dominate Brussels brewing, and in doing so proved its downfall. Of the stars of 1958 only Wiel's Pils of the Wielemans-Ceuppens brewery survived, but by the early '80s even its shine had dimmed substantially.

R.S.C. ANDERLECHT 81-82
CHAMPION DE BELGIQUE 80-81 KAMPIOEN VAN BELGIE 80-81
GUEUZE BELLE·VUE

#32
'81-'82 Anderlecht Team Photo
1981

- City Life

In Brussels, the defining debate that splits the city - setting neighbour against neighbour - isn't about beer. It's about football. Do you wear the red-white-black of Molenbeek, Royale Union St Gilloise's yellow-and-blue, or the mauve of Anderlecht. Union - who don't play in St Gilles but in next-door Vorst - were all-conquering before WWII, racking up 11 league titles. In the late-1930s, they had a young local playing up front, a brewer's son who later moved across town to play for the *Paars-wit* of Anderlecht before his career was truncated by injury and wartime family tragedy.

Constant Vanden Stock never forgot his footballing origins, even when he was forced to leave the game to run Brasserie Belle-Vue following his father's death. "Anyone who looks closely enough at my forehead," Vanden Stock said, talking later to writer Hugo Camps, "can still see the imprint of the laces." After exchanging his boots for a brewer's smock, he maintained his links with his first love throughout the 1960s. While guiding Belle-Vue to its dominant position as Brussels' largest Lambic brewery, Vanden Stock continued coaching and was appointed the selector for the Belgian men's national team. In his absence Anderlecht, like Belle-Vue, prospered in the 1960s, winning a record five straight titles. But by decade's end, financial issues forced the club to approach their former player for investment. In 1969 Vanden Stock joined Anderlecht's board, bringing 450,000 francs with him. Within two years he assumed total control.

Involvement in sport was not unusual for Brussels' breweries. In the same period, Wielemans-Ceuppens sponsored the Groene Leeuw cycling team. But Vanden Stock's investment in Anderlecht was different, and his tenure mirrored his work at Belle-Vue: domestic consolidation followed by adventures in Europe. He excised the dead wood from the playing squad, and reorganised the club's parlous finances and woeful infrastructure.

A league and cup double followed in 1972. In 1973, the circular Belle-Vue logo arrived on Anderlecht's purple-and-white jerseys, where it would stay as team sponsor for the rest of the decade. Vanden Stock's "most beautiful [football] memory" came in 1976 when Anderlecht beat West Ham 4-2 to lift the UEFA Cup Winners' Cup in Brussels. A second Cup Winners' Cup followed in 1978, another league title in 1981, as Anderlecht and Belle-Vue conquered all-comers.

The team lining up for the next season's group photo had been shaped by Vanden Stock into a formidable force. There was Juan Lozano, the Spanish midfielder seated fifth from the right who Vanden Stock called an "unsurpassed artist". Standing at the back, sporting a bouffant mullet, was Ludo Coeck, a winger pairing "class and intelligence with a rare elegance." Anderlecht didn't win anything that season, but a year later they hoisted another European trophy. Belle-Vue's shirt sponsorship had by this time been replaced by the Generale Bank. But when Anderlecht's players lined out to play a friendly match against Diego Maradona's F.C. Barcelona in August 1983 they did so under the floodlights of the remodelled, and newly-baptised Constant Vanden Stock stadium.

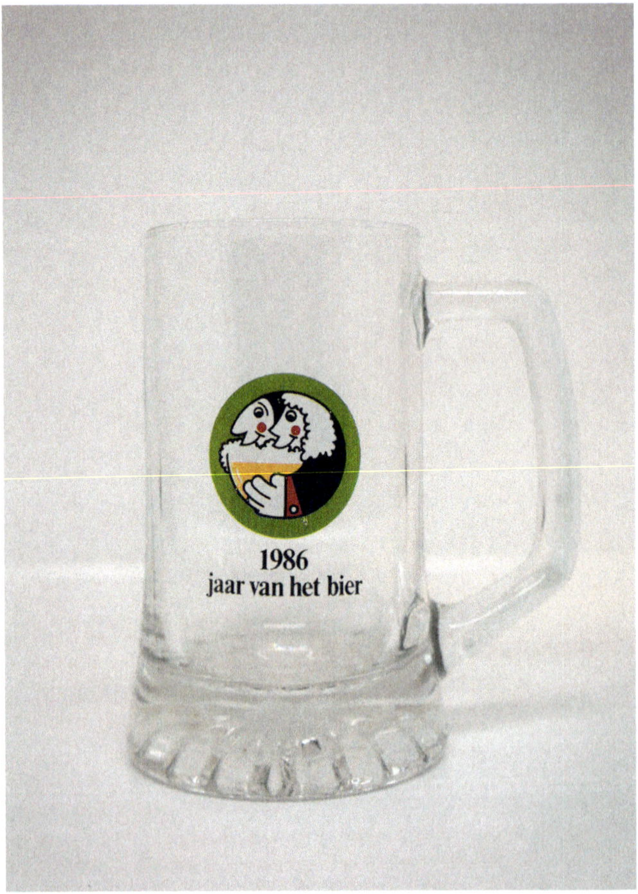
1986
jaar van het bier

#33

Jaar Van Het Bier Tankard

1986

- Business Life

In 1986, Belgium's politico-brewing complex met in Brussels. Sitting at a table strewn with pastries and flyers was a fresh-faced (and future Belgian Prime Minister) Guy Verhofstadt. Though more a wine-drinker, the then-budget minister paid due deference to his brewer hosts, declaring: "Every minister should, as much as they can, strive to support that which gives so much pride and pleasure to our country."

On his left sat Paul de Keersmaecker, agriculture minister and former brewer at his family's Mort Subite brewery. On Verhofstadt's right sat Wilfried Martens, then-Prime Minister and in agreement with his junior colleague's opinion on beer. "Like any self-respecting Belgian," Martens said, "occasionally I drink a pint." Behind this trio crowded the massed ranks of Belgium's brewing establishment, decked out in the robes, medallions, and floppy hats of their brewers' guild.

Their meeting could have been mistaken for a wake, such was the parlous state of Belgian brewing in 1986. Belgians drank less beer - down from 131 litres per person in 1980 to 121 by 1985. There were fewer breweries too, their number collapsing from a post-

WWII total of over 600, to 126 in the mid-'80s.

Brussels would have been an excellent venue for a wake. The city's once-thriving brewery community was decimated by the impact first of industrialisation, then the privations of successive world wars, and finally the commodification, de-industrialisation, and suburbanisation of the later 20th century.

By 1986 there were only three breweries left in Brussels. One, Belle-Vue, was inching its way towards a purpose-built Lambic factory in Flanders. Another, Brasserie Cantillon, survived by converting itself into a working museum to a brewing culture it alone now represented. The third, Brasserie Wielemans-Ceuppens, was now owned by the Artois brewery, haemorrhaging money and operating under the close surveillance of beancounters in Leuven.

But Verhofstadt and co. weren't there to deliver Belgian beer's last rites. Because what once looked like a terminal case was - at least outside Brussels - showing signs of life. As a contemporaneous brewery guide explained, in the early 1980s hundreds of new beers emerged onto Belgium's beer scene. Some were regional beers receiving wider distribution, others "rediscovered" old recipes, and yet more completely new - like Boon in Lembeek, De Dolle Brouwers in West Flanders, or Wallonia's Brasserie d'Achouffe.

The politicians and brewers hoped to invigorate this revival by delivering a defibrillating shock to the beer industry in the form of the *Jaar van het Bier* ("Year of Beer") - a year-long celebration featuring new beer-centric books, new beers, and events across the country culminating in a Brouwersfeest beer festival on Brussels' Grand Place in October 1986.

And it worked, sort of. The number of breweries eventually bottomed out at 121 in 1989, before rising again. Pils remained dominant, though the production of so-called "speciaalbieren", Trappist, and abbey beers had grown from 12.8% in 1985 to 21.5% by 1992. But Gueuze and Lambic - Brussels' indigenous beers - consumption went in the opposite direction, and for Belgium's capital city, the worst was yet to come.

A History of Brussels Beer in 50 Objects

144

#34

Musée De La Bière Schaerbeekois Beer Mats

1994

- City Life

The '70s and early '80s were turbulent for Brussels' brewers, with closure after closure thinning their numbers. But the sector reached its real low ebb in the early 1990s. The end of Vorst's Brasserie Wielemans-Ceuppens in 1988 left Lambic-producing Brasserie Belle-Vue as Brussels' last remaining industrial brewery. In 1991 Wielemans' owners Interbrew, Belgium's biggest brewery, took control of Belle-Vue. Within five years they'd cease brewing at their Molenbeek brewery, leaving nearby Brasserie Cantillon as the last Brussels brewery standing.

March 1994 seems, then, like an inauspicious moment for the arrival in the city of the *Musée de la Bière Schaerbeekois*. The beer enthusiasts and collectors behind the project could have been forgiven for thinking that, rather than a museum celebrating Brussels' (and Belgium's) beer heritage, they were about to open a mausoleum to a recently-deceased culture. Schaarbeek would have been a good choice for either endeavour. Home in the early 1900s to 13 breweries and cherry orchards producing fruit for Brussels' *Kriekenlambiek*, by the 1990s all that was left of this tradition was *L'Ordre de la Griotte*, a society honouring the neighbourhood's cherry harvesters founded by local alderman Claude Paulet.

Paulet was also involved in the museum. He secured a location in the former ateliers of an abandoned technical school not far from Schaarbeek's Josaphat park, where the museum's founders could install their collection of Belgian breweriana and brewery equipment. In early 1994 burly men in sweat-soaked shirts heaved bottling machines and brewing kettles into various rooms, and in the main exhibition area they placed a Wielemans dray cart complete with red livery, beer barrels, and a dummy in the driver's seat.

Another room was converted into the *Vieux Schaerbeek* ("Old Schaarbeek"), recreating a classic 1920s Brussels estaminet, featuring games like *pitjesbak*, and *vogelpik*, a royal decree from November 1939 outlawing drunkenness, a charcoal stove, and a pair of mannequins (one a notary, the other his mistress) sitting down for a bottle of Gueuze Belle-Vue.

Shelves were filled with thousands of bottles and beer glasses from breweries around Belgium. In glass cabinets were placed yellowing newspaper ads, beer label stencils, coasters, tap handles topped with golden elephants, brewer's medallions, and share certificates from long-defunct Brussels breweries. On the walls they affixed enamel advertisements and the backlit electric signs that replaced them. In one corner was a library, featuring old copies of *Le Petit Brasseur* announcing the death of Louis Pasteur. In another they installed a small bar serving their house beer - called *Schaerbeekoise* but made, in the absence of local breweries, 95 kilometres away at Brasserie de l'Abbaye des Rocs.

Much of the museum's collection was already distant history in 1994, and it hasn't shaken off its melancholic air in subsequent years. But it hasn't quite been suspended in aspic. The volunteers have continued growing their collection to reflect Belgium's late-20th century beer revival. And these days the museum café can even offer visitors a glass of Brussels-brewed beer - their *Eizelskop* tripel coming from Nanobrasserie L'Ermitage in slightly less distant Anderlecht.

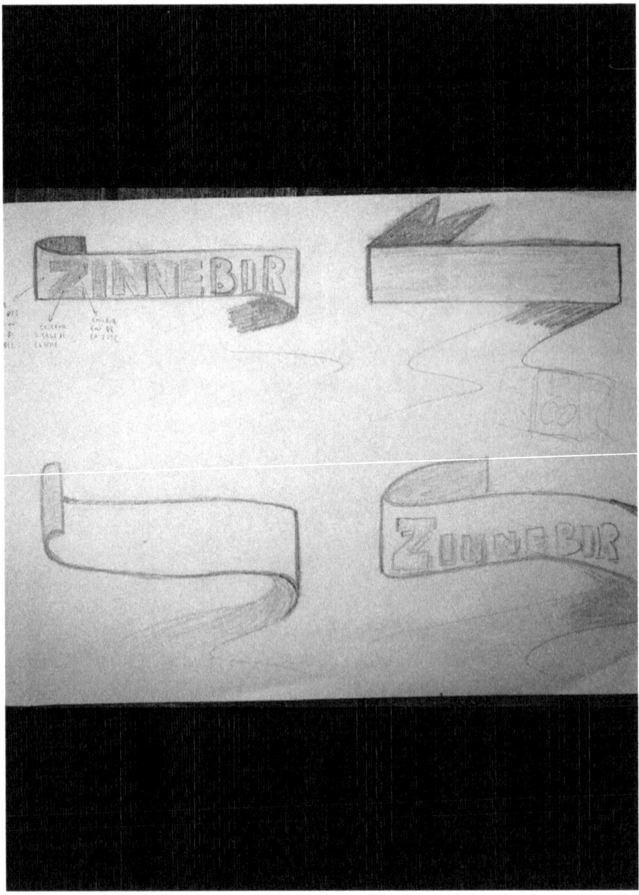
ZINNEBIR
ZINNEBIR

#35

Sketches for a Zinnebir Label

2002-2006

- Brewery Life

Bernard Leboucq was no illustrator. Given his job at Brasserie de la Senne was primarily brewing beer, that wasn't much of an issue.

Brasserie de la Senne's origin story is a well-trodden tale. In early 2002 Leboucq was homebrewing in the basement of a squat, providing a beer called Zinnebir for the second edition of the Zinneke Parade - a biennial festival celebrating Brussels' diverse neighbourhoods and multicultural population. It was on the margins of the festival that a fateful meet-cute occurred between Leboucq and Yvan De Baets, a fellow Brussellaar and a youth-focused social worker with a keen interest in brewing and beer history.

Within a year Leboucq had started a brewery - the *Sint-Pietersbrouwerij* - in a Flemish suburb just outside Brussels, an earlier plan of his to open a brewery in Ixelles having failed to materialise. De Baets became Leboucq's *de facto* technical consultant until 2006, when together they launched Brasserie de la Senne. Brewing by necessity in various locations around Belgium, the pair maintained their connection with their home city, always harbouring the wish to return and featuring Brussels iconography heavily in their new brewery's identity.

Hand-drawn by Leboucq in ink on brown craft paper, the earliest Zinnebir labels featured a muddy illustration of the Zenne river, and "Zinnebir" in big bold lettering. Zinnebir itself was more refined, taking inspiration from the early-20th century Belgian Pale Ale (or *Spéciale Belge*) tradition, but diverging from this amber, malty template in favour of something, according to De Baets, "drier, hoppier and more bitter". Their Zinnebir was also a reaction to the dark, sweet, heavy beers dominating mainstream Belgian brewing in the early 2000s. Instead, it channelled de la Senne's twin influences of English cask ales that married complexity with drinkability, and *Mitteleuropa*'s noble hop tradition.

It was a successful formula. This assertively bitter (for Belgium) beer and its stablemates filtered out of Brussels, eventually making it to an American beer importer who expressed an interest in Zinnebir, on one condition: new, more attractive labels.

Fortunately for Leboucq, help was close at hand. His cousin, Jean Goovaerts, happened to be a trained artist and comics illustrator. Leboucq was soon on the phone to him. "[Bernard] said, 'I'm in a mess, you need to help me!',' Goovaerts recalls. After a few hours doodling and what Goovaerts calls "automatic creation", they came up with a new design inspired in part by Art Deco and Goovaerts' love of Russian suprematism and the modernist aesthetic of interwar political posters.

The Zenne was retained, but transformed from black

into a bright green stream winding its way between cubist buildings towards lettering proclaiming "Zinnebir: A Brussels People's Ale" and a golden-yellow stylised sunrise. It was an optimistic image, foreshadowing the coming rebirth of brewing in Brussels and an optimistic future de la Senne was about to embark on - even if the brewery was to spend the rest of the decade in nomadic exile from Brussels, biding their time for the chance to return to their spiritual home.

A History of Brussels Beer in 50 Objects

#36
Moeder Lambic Serviette
2006

- Pub Life

In this edition of the Brussels beer New Testament, the role of John the Baptist will be played by Frenchman Jean Hummler. Now, I can already hear dissenting voices suggesting other, more appropriate figures who foretold - and helped usher in - Brussels beer renaissance. Surely, someone might say, Yvan De Baets and Bernard Leboucq have as much a claim as Hummler, given their Brasserie de la Senne opened the same year Hummler and his business partners took control of the Chez Moeder Lambic beer café.

But go back further than 2006, all the way to the 1980s, and another candidate emerges - the man who founded the original iteration of Moeder Lambic. Joël Pêcheur opened Chez Moeder Lambic on November 5, 1983. Within three years a Brussels beer café guidebook proclaimed it as having, with an 800-beers long menu featuring beers from China, Ireland, and Zaire, "the largest choice of beers in the whole of Brabant." Shortly afterwards Pêcheur took this template, with its comic book reading nook, beer and onion soup, and "must drink" Blanche, and opened a second branch four kilometres away in Brussels' university district.

Pêcheur's conception of a beer bar focused on breadth, and a mid-1980s Moeder Lambic menu might have featured Hoegaarden and Peroni alongside the likes of Anchor, Budweiser, and Guinness. Later, having left Moeder Lambic in the mid-1990s, it was a formula Pêcheur would perfect at a more central location in Brussels, when he returned to the hospitality industry in 2003 to open the Delirium Tremens bar.

By that time Moeder Lambic had changed too, gradually shifting away from a broad industrial menu towards more independent-spirited beers from the likes of Brouwerij De Ranke. When Hummler and his business partners Andy Mengal and Nassim Dessicy took over the lease for Moeder Lambic in 2006, they were determined to continue on this path.

Theirs was a vision of a beer bar that didn't try to cover all the bases but instead committed itself assertively - sometimes pugnaciously - to supporting small, local, and independent breweries producing characterful, quality beers. That meant, for example, calling on Jean Van Roy of Cantillon and asking him to provide a Kriek they could serve through a traditional beer machine. And it meant standing up to the legal department of Belgian brewery Duvel when it threatened, according to Hummler in an interview with the Belgian Smaak podcast recorded in 2017, to throttle their business if they didn't maintain the business relationship of Moeder Lambic's previous tenants.

It was, in the Brussels of 2006, an unproven concept. But within three years they had opened their own second outlet in central Brussels and by Moeder Lambic's 10th anniversary it - and de la Senne - had been joined in the city by a host of new breweries and beercentric bars that shared their commitment to localism and independence. In the second decade of the 21st century, it was not Pêcheur's iteration of Moeder Lambic but Hummler's that formed the ideological basis of Brussels' nascent beer revival.

A History of Brussels Beer in 50 Objects

#37
Around Brussels in 80 Beers
2009

- Pub Life

In 2009 "Around Brussels in 80 Beers" was published by an old Belgian beer hand. Written by Joe Stange, a young(ish) American reporter, and brewer Yvan De Baets, the concept was simple: 80 good bars matched with 80 good beers. A Brussels beer guide was nothing new; local politician Sven Gatz had published his own guide to 101 bars in 2002. But, arriving in the wake of Moeder Lambic's revival and ahead of Brasserie de la Senne's return to Brussels, "Around..." added to a feeling that the decades-long decline of Brussels' beer was over.

Joe explains, briefly, how the book came to be:

An idea

"A freelance gig had ended, and my attempts at writing fiction were hilariously bad. So I started writing what I hoped would be a proper guidebook to finding great beer in Brussels. Obviously, going to a bunch of beer cafés sounded like an ideal way to pass the time. And it was."

Inspiration

"My starting point was Tim [Webb]'s Good Beer Guide (GBG) Belgium. I held it and Tim's work in very high regard. When somebody told me - it might have been Tim himself - he was planning a Brussels guide, my first thought was, "Well fuck it, I can't compete with that." So I nearly quit... Instead, I rang Tim up on February 3, 2008. I told him I'd been working on something similar, strongly implying he should probably just let me write his book."

The pitch

"The next day, I followed up by email with...this:

> *'Your [GBG] chapter on Brussels is the best thing available at the moment, but clearly there's room for something more devoted to the city and its unique culture. So many pubs here have interesting stories that connect in some way with the city's history. Meanwhile, with so many bars in the city—good and bad—there's a real chance to steer people toward interesting beers, instead of more of the same. I know a lot of expats...and we host plenty of tourists. Nearly all are asking for at least two things: great beer and guidance.'*

A co-author

"I learned from Tim he'd already been talking to Yvan about writing the book. There was obvious appeal in combining Yvan's deep local expertise (and great taste) with an English-speaking writer/editor. As a bonus, I had no day job...and loads of time to wander around... getting lost down rabbit holes of Brussels history and beery esoterica. [Yvan] had plenty of suggestions to help fill out and improve our list of 80 cafés, and plenty of the kinds of strong opinions that can give a guidebook the edge it ought to have."

Launching at Brasserie Cantillon

"I don't remember much. Mainly, I was really proud to be standing there with Tim and Yvan. And, I didn't feel as young as I looked. Then [it] was incredibly successful and we all got rich. The end."

Postscript - *Tim Webb*: "Definitely try that fiction writing thing. I especially liked the ending, 'We all got incredibly rich.'"

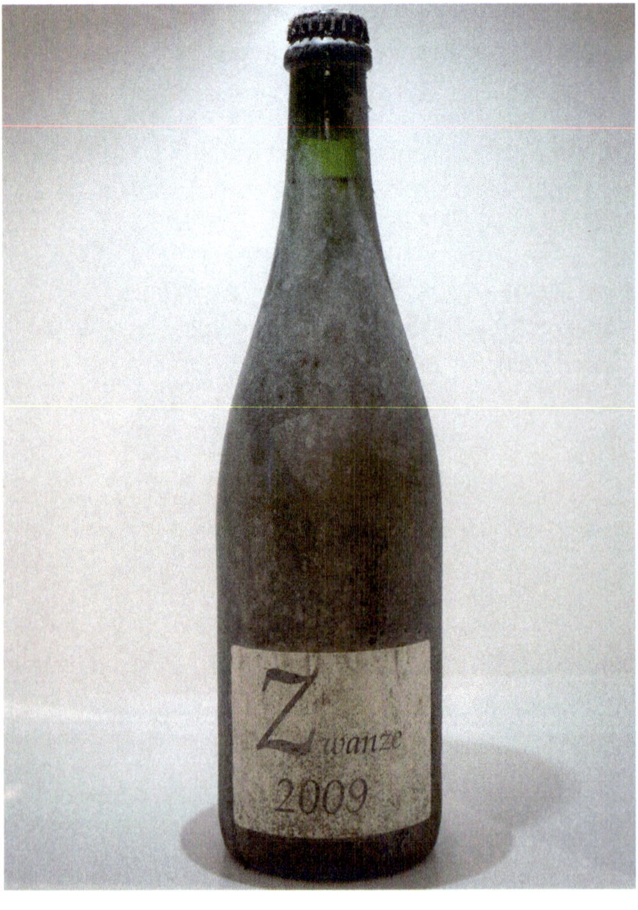
Zwanze
2009

#38
Zwanze 2009
2009

- Brewery Life

On Saturday November 7, 2009, Brasserie Cantillon launched a new beer. Christened Zwanze 2009, it was a very limited-run Lambic aged with hand-picked elderflower. A brewery releasing a new beer is nothing exceptional - even if said brewery is Cantillon, makes Lambic, and works on a timescale of years rather than months and weeks like conventional breweries. This wasn't even the first Cantillon Zwanze, that honour having been given a year previously to a rhubarb-infused Lambic. But 2009 was an auspicious year for Cantillon, and 2009's Zwanze an auspicious beer - one prefiguring a decade of Lambic growth, experimentation, and covetous-bordering-on-obsessive fan culture.

Zwanze is a child of Brussels' working-class neighbourhoods, a bawdy and knowing sense of humour, sometimes impenetrable to outsiders. Zwanze 2008's label gives an example, of sorts: "A Lambic with vegetables? That's true *Zwanze*!" Jean Van Roy, Cantillon's owner, wanted to experiment with some Lambic heterodoxy - hence the rhubarb and elderflower - and *Zwanze* was useful shorthand. "The idea of this [beer] is to do...fun tests around Lambic without taking ourselves too seriously," he said when launching 2009's Zwanze. (*Zwanze* would later also land them in trouble for a crude and ill-judged cabaret performance in 2018, parts of which the brewery later said were a "huge mistake".)

2009 saw the 40th anniversary of Jean-Pierre Van Roy taking over Cantillon from his father-in-law, and marked 30 years since Jean's joining him. It also witnessed Van Roy *père* mashing in for his final Lambic brew. That Van Roy *fils* was now able to flirt with Lambic *zwanzen* was down to Jean-Pierre's hard graft. He rescued the brewery in the late 1970s, spent the next decade keeping it solvent, and subsequent years nurturing it to profitability.

Jean inherited a business that, having skirted oblivion, was entitled to indulge in a little frivolity. So there was rhubarb and elderflower Zwanze Lambics, and later a spontaneous witbier and "Wild Brussels Stout". However experimental they were, they were no less successful than the brewery's standard fare. Zwanze 2008 and 2009 would become semi-regular fixtures in Cantillon's line-up as, respectively, Nath and Mamouche. There has since been more experimentation, under the Zwanze appellation but also in the brewery's deepening exploration of, and comingling with, viniculture.

By Zwanze 2010's release, bottles were leaking onto the black market, causing Jean to complain, ahead of Zwanze 2011, that "[u]nfortunately, there are those… who couldn't care less about spontaneous fermentation beer but who do care a lot about making easy money." His response was Zwanze Day: a now-annual, globally-synchronised release of that year's beer. It celebrated Lambic's phoenix-like revival from the 20th century's deathly ashes, together with the businesses who helped it happen.

But a shift was underway in Lambic. As the Zenne valley's spontaneous fermentation beers gained a global following, Lambic was becoming decontextualised from its *heimat*, from the anachronistic traditions that spoke to drinkers' unarticulated yearning for a pre-modern idyll. Slowly, a new culture was emerging, identified by an acquisitive obsession with rarity, the influence of which was no joke.

BRUSSELS CALLING
(BITTER IS BETTER)
BRASSERIE DE LA SENNE
MADE IN BRUSSELS BELGIUM
BIOLOGISCH BIER / ORGANIC BEER
BELGIAN
IPA

#39
Brussels Calling
2010

- Brewery Life

Ritual - sometimes sacred, sometimes profane, usually a heady mixture of both - has always been central to Brussels' beer culture. The city's medieval brewers' guild held meetings in their Grand Place guildhall under the dual patronages of St Arnoldus and King Gambrinus, and were active participants in the torchlit royal processions, Ommegang pageants, and religious feasts of the period. Brussels' brewing season, like much of pre-modern northern Europe, began and ended on saints' days - stretching from the feast of St Michael on September 29 to St George's Day on April 23 in early spring.

These days the rituals lean more profane than sacred. The country's brewers still gather in the old guildhall, marking the arrival of autumn (and the start of the Belgian Beer Weekend festival) by traipsing from the Grand Place up the Treurenberg hill to Brussels' cathedral for a mass in St Arnoldus' honour. Lambic brewing still takes place during winter, though now it's book-ended not by religious observances but by public brew days at Brasserie Cantillon.

As Brussels' long-dormant brewing sector began

waking up towards the end of the 2000s, the brewers and drinkers responsible for its revival introduced their own rituals. The first of these arrived on the afternoon of December 22, 2010. On that day, Brasserie de la Senne brewed the inaugural batch of beer at their new Brussels brewery housed in an old industrial bakery adjoining the Molenbeek cemetery. This test batch announced the end of the brewery's near decade-long nomadic trek across Flanders, Wallonia and France, and its return to its hometown city. It also marked the opening of Brussels' first new brewery in decades, instantly doubling from one to two the number of commercial breweries in the city and signalling a turning point in its brewing history.

Having searched for a location in Brussels for several years, by 2009 it looked like de la Senne had found it - a 1,000-square metre location in Molenbeek enabling them to double the amount of beer they made. By winter 2010 de la Senne had moved in, and were sure that the beer with which they planned to test their new brewhouse would be special.

Not veering too far from the template that had served the brewery so well thus far, they took the Taras Boulba formula - light, dry, bitter - and increased the ABV a little and used German Hallertaü Hersbrucker hops. De la Senne christened it Brussels Calling, designated it as a Belgian IPA, and released the beer early in 2011.

It's a ritual Brasserie de la Senne has observed every December since. The brewery might tweak the recipe each year, with Herkules hops used in 2013, for example, and Hallertau Blanc in 2014. But every year, as the vernal equinox approaches, a beer called Brussels Calling starts appearing on shelves and in glasses across the city, foamy and effervescent and burnished yellow and announcing, as it did the year before, that the dark winter is nearly over and spring is just around the corner.

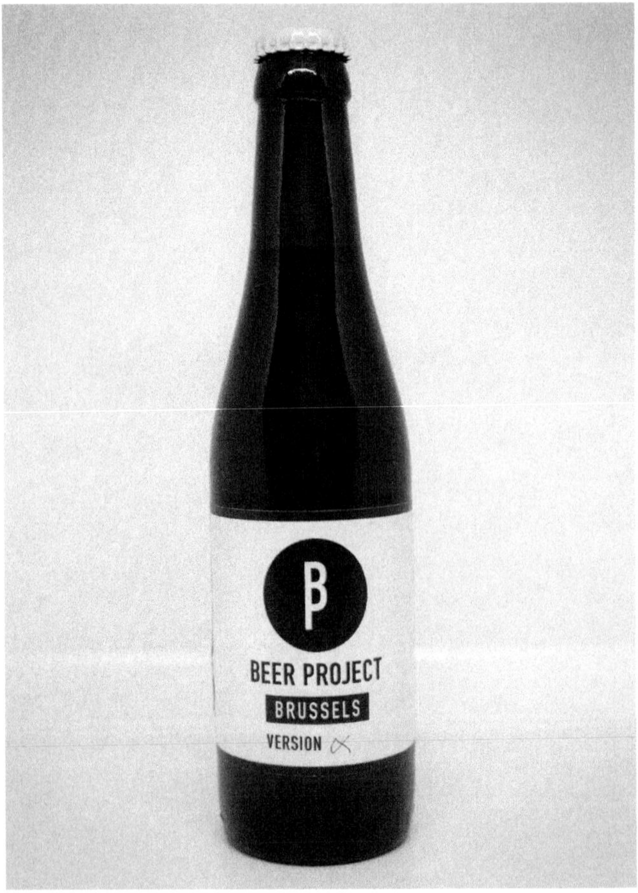
BEER PROJECT
BRUSSELS
VERSION

#40
Brussels Beer Project Alpha
2013

- Brewery Life

"Why should every beer come from the middle ages?" With this question, Brussels Beer Project (BBP) announced its arrival in May 2013 as Brussels' first self-consciously "craft" beer producer. Where Cantillon was a multi-generational family brewery, and Brasserie de la Senne a modern brewery re-interpreting older traditions, BBP were different.

Its founders, Sébastien Morvan and Olivier de Brauwere, met at university in Canada, discovering a shared interest in beer. Quite deliberately, BBP didn't sound like Brussels' established breweries either, though their projection of a self-consciously counter-corporate ethos would have been familiar to craft beer drinkers in bars from Brooklyn to Bermondsey. BBP's beers were different too. More interesting than the origin of the beers - they were brewed at the Limburg-based Brouwerij Anders - was how they were chosen.

BBP's model was a participatory one. A Mad Max Beyond Thunderdome-esque slogan - "4 prototypes. 1 will survive" - introduced their central idea: they would present to drinkers, over a month-long series of tastings across Brussels, four prototype beers developed with Anders. A public vote would then decide which became their first core beer.

Each prototype received a Greek letter and a colour. The beers were similar - pale and bitter - with the recipes varying in the quantity and variety of spices, hops, or yeast used. Blue Alpha was brewed with Smaragd hops, coriander and orange peel, and was described as a bitter and fruity Belgian Pale Ale. Yellow Beta was an amber-red farmhouse-style blonde made with paradise seeds, juniper berries, and saison yeast. Red Gamma was another Pale Ale, featuring cardamom & candy sugar. Green Delta, came with the tagline "[s]mells like heaven, bitter as hell", a Belgian IPA brewed with Smaragd and Citra hops.

The final tasting took place on the last Saturday in June 2013, in the old machine room of Brasserie Wielemans-Ceuppens. 855 people voted and the winner, with 303, was Delta. Shortly thereafter BBP announced a crowd-sourced competition to give the beer a new name. But before announcing the winner, in September 2013 they launched their first crowdfunding campaign, Beer For Life, raising €50,000 from 369 contributors. Then came a new beer in January 2014, Dark Sister, and a second crowdsourced beer, the Belgian Hefeweizen called Grosse Bertha. In October 2015, BBP opened their city-centre brewery on Rue Antoine Dansaert. More crowdsourced beers and Beers For Life campaigns followed, alongside bars in Tokyo (2017) and Paris (2018 and 2019).

And in early 2022, BBP cranked into action their new

"Port Sud" brewery on the canal in Anderlecht, allowing them to bring all their brewing in-house for the first time. The first beer piped into the brand-new fermentation tanks had changed a little since its 2013 debut. It was now a Saison IPA, dropped half a degree in alcohol, and now came packaged in cans. But the cans were still green (albeit with an orange sash), and the beer was still called Delta. Because, in Brussels Beer Project's decade-long dash, they never did quite get around to giving it a new name.

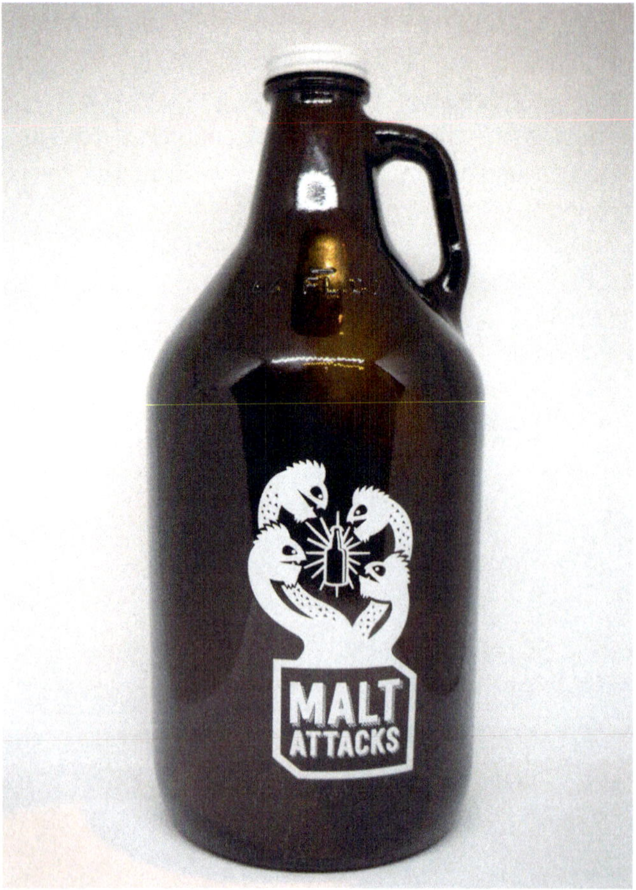
MALT
ATTACKS

#41
Malt Attacks Growler
2014

- Pub Life

There's a scene partway through Luc Besson's *The Fifth Element* where the film's oleaginous antagonist Jean-Baptiste Emanuel Zorg monologues to Ian Holm's priest about his belief that life comes from "destruction, disorder and chaos" - illustrating his point by smashing a glass, prompting an army of robots into life to clean up the mess.

The five decades of destruction, disorder and chaos visited on Brussels' beer scene in the late 20th century may have been down more to callous indifference than deliberate malice. But deliberate or not, by the early 2010s decline had finally given way to a hubbub of activity. A new beer ecosystem was emerging into the vacuum left behind by the disappearance of Brussels' industrial breweries.

There were new beer-curious restaurants, rumours of new breweries, and homebrewers with ambitions to escape their basements. People like Kevin Desmet (a.k.a the Belgian Beer Geek) were writing about the embryonic scene, and there was renewed interest in brewing courses at the Institut Meurice and COOVI. And in October 2014 a small beer shop opened down the hill from the Parvis de St Gilles.

Identifiable by the four-headed hydra painted on the shop-window, Malt Attacks was owned by history graduate Antoine Pierson. It was small, with room for twin sets of black shelves flanking a counter in the middle. The beers Pierson placed on these shelves retrospectively feels like a capsule collection of what interesting beer looked like in 2014. One side housed the Belgians - locals Cantillon and Brasserie de la Senne but also St Bernardus, De Glazen Toren, Dupont, Fantôme, Rulles, and De Struise Brouwers.

On the opposite wall was everyone else. American standards like Sierra Nevada Pale Ale and Anchor Steam, and more niche bottles from the likes of Prairie Artisan Ales and The Bruery. From England there was Fuller's Vintage Ale, Weird Beard, Brew By Numbers, and The Kernel. Scandinavia was well represented, with Norway's Nogne Ø having a shelf almost to itself alongside Brouwerij De Molen of The Netherlands, and boxes of BrewDog.

Malt Attacks wasn't Brussels' first craft beer shop - Ixelles-based Malting Pot opened in 2014 - but it had a unique selling point, which even in 2014 had a whiff of exoticism to it: it sold growlers of freshly-tapped beers for takeaway. But it's not the availability of draught Bastogne Pale Ale or Nøgne Ø's Two Captains Double IPA that make Malt Attacks' arrival so significant, for me at least. When it opened, I lived a few streets away, a new dad with a burgeoning interest in beer. Malt Attacks felt then like the Brussels outpost of an international beer movement of which I was still only dimly aware. It was where, for example, I bought my first Sierra Nevada and my first Punk IPA in November 2014.

For many beer drinkers, Malt Attacks was an essential conduit between a sometimes-insular Brussels and an outside world just then exploding with interesting beer. And as its emissary in Brussels, Antoine Pierson was the perfect honorary consul.

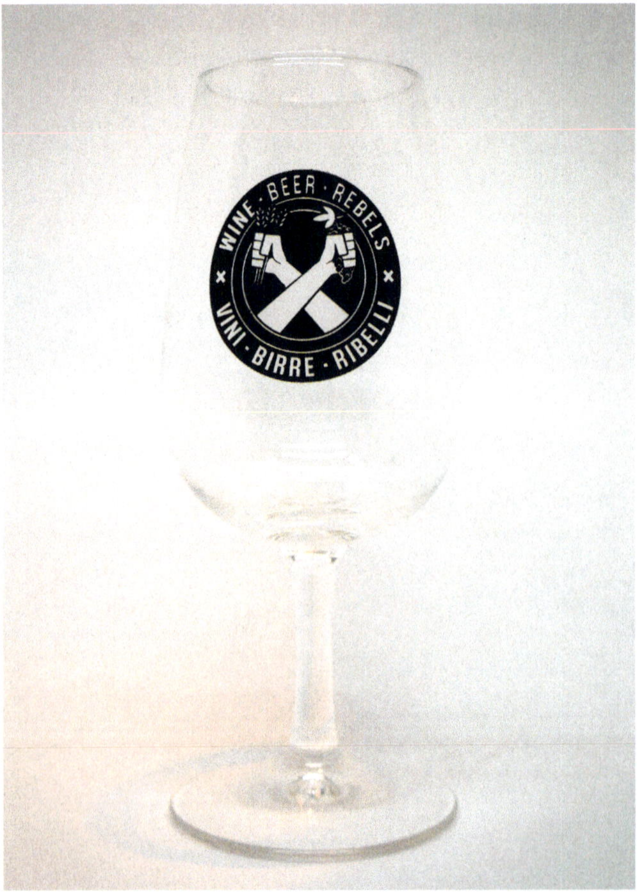
WINE · BEER · REBELS
VINI · BIRRE · RIBELLI

#42

Vini Birre Ribelli Glass

2014

- City Life

Vini Birre Ribelli arrived like a bolt from the blue in Brussels, and disappeared almost as suddenly. Running from 2014 to 2017, this beer-and-wine festival was short-lived, but its influence on Brussels' beer scene was long-lasting.

As its name suggests, Vini Birre Ribelli had Italophile leanings and focused on unconventional or unusual producers. In 2014, this was not an idea completely out of left-field; Brussels' beer community has long had close relations with its Italian counterparts - evidenced by Moeder Lambic's regular Italian tap takeovers, Brasserie Cantillon's close relationship with Italian winemakers, and restaurants like the Roman La Tana. Vini Birre Ribelli's first edition in December 2014 featured wines from Piedmont, Emilia-Romagna, and Tuscany, and beers from Fidenza's Toccalmatto and LoverBeer and Montegioco of Piedmont. There was also local representation in the form of Brasserie Cantillon, Tilquin, and others.

Housed in the Maison De la Poste building at the Tour & Taxis former industrial site, Vini Birre Ribelli was founded by Moeder Lambic's Jean Hummler, Italian sommelier Enrico D'Ambrogio, wine writer Patrick Böttcher, and cultural administrator Caroline Vermeulen. It was not Brussels' first beer festival, the Belgian Beer Weekend having occupied the Grand Place on the last weekend of August annually since the early 2000s. And nine years before Vini Birre Ribelli's appearance, Brasserie de la Senne organised the first edition (of four) of their Bruxellensis "characterful beer" festival featuring beers the likes of De Ranke, Thiriez from Northern France, and England's Ramsgate brewery.

But like Bruxellensis, Vini Birre Ribelli's lifespan was truncated. In 2015 it decamped to the Koning Boudewijn stadium before returning to the canal neighbourhood in 2016 and 2017, first to an abandoned Citroën garage on Ijzerplein, then back to Tour & Taxis in November 2017 for a fourth edition. There was to be no fifth edition. But beer drinkers need not have worried, because 2017 turned out to be a bit of a landmark year for Brussels beer festivals.

Hummler had already by then a new project, launching the BXLBeerfest that August with restaurateur Olivier Desmet, Kevin Desmet of Belgian Beer Geek, and journalist Vincent Callut - in the exact same location as Vini Birre Ribelli's final edition. In June 2017 the brains behind Malt Attacks, Barboteur in Schaarbeek, and St Gilles' Dynamo held their own festival, SWAFFF, in Schaarbeek. Later, they would cross the canal to a renovated farmhouse in Molenbeek. Like BXLBeerfest and Vini Birre Ribelli, SWAFFF featured established and up-and-coming Belgian breweries alongside a mix of continental and UK breweries like Norwegian Lervig, Estonian Pohjala, and London's Anspach & Hobday. In October, they were joined by Brussels Beer Project's Wanderlust.

These new festivals, while possessing their own aesthetic, shared some similarities. A focus on small, independent, and interesting producers. Taking food seriously - sometimes even roping some of Brussels' biggest culinary stars. And their location on or near Brussels' canal, confirming the inexorable shift westward of Brussels beer's centre of gravity. All of which Vini Birre Ribelli did first.

Vini Birre Ribelli is dead. Long live Vini Birre Ribelli.

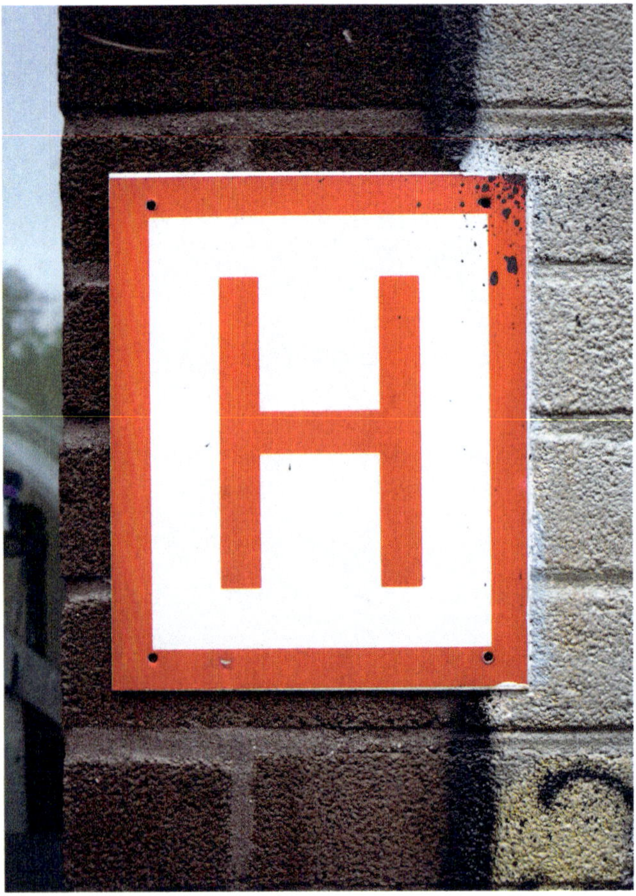
H

#43

Rue du Miroir 1

2015

- Brewery Life

I lost my journalistic virginity at Rue de Miroir 1. On a balmy Wednesday evening in early July 2017, I met Denys Van Elewyck of Brasserie En Stoemelings for my very first interview for Brussels Beer City.

Denys (an archaeology graduate) founded the brewery with his friend Samuel Languy (a computer game developer) in 2013, brewing first in cellars and family kitchens before graduating to a professional kitchen at a co-working office in east Brussels. The brewery's name, Denys said, came from these early, furtive brews: "When we first began to brew it was…in a basement without windows…[En Stoemelings] means the way we did things, in a secret way, behind the curtain, under the table."

Their first commercial beer was Curieuse Neus (translating roughly as "Nosy Parker"), a Tripel, and traditional Belgian styles would become their trademark. But before they could increase the number and variety of beers they brewed, they needed a proper home. That is what led them, in 2015, to the empty space on the edge of Brussels' Marollen neighbourhood where I would eventually meet Denys. It was impractically small, barely big enough to house En Stoemelings' plastic fermentation tanks, oversized gas hobs and large pots-cum-brewing vessels. But as a symbol, it was huge.

Brussels' *pentagone* hadn't been home to a commercial brewery since the 1950s, and hadn't seen a new brewery since the city's interbellum brewing heyday. What's more, En Stoemelings' new home was only a couple of streets over from Albert Vossen's Mort Subite Lambic blendery, and where construction workers purportedly "discovered" the original manuscript of *Les Mémoires de Jef lambic* hidden in a beer barrel.

But by the time of my sheepish interview in 2017, Denys' attention was already elsewhere and I wasn't the only one embarking on a new adventure. That En Stoemelings had outgrown their first home and its 205 litre brew kit was clear to me as I sat with Denys at the brewery's makeshift bar, surrounded by boxes, brewing paraphernalia and bottles both empty and full.

That was why I was there too, to record En Stoemelings' final days in the Marollen before they jumped the canal to a new, larger home in a semi-industrial complex adjacent to Tour and Taxis. They were abandoning their hand-cranked bottling machine in favour of stainless steel from Slovenia and, Denys said that evening, it was not before time. Their cramped brewery wasn't just inconvenient, it was actively hindering their growth as brewers and En Stoemelings' as a business: "You can stay, stay, stay, but as we say in French, it's *mourir dans l'oeuf* – dead before it's born."

By November they'd escaped their egg and were relearning how to brew on their new equipment. After our early, anxiety-inducing encounter, my own little clandestine project had avoided an early death too. 12 months later I would meet Denys again - this time at their new digs, he an increasingly confident brewer at a flourishing En Stoemelings, and me inching ever-closer towards competence as an interviewer.

A History of Brussels Beer in 50 Objects

#44

Pistolet Original Belgian Hot Dog

2016

- Food Life

Parisian writer Gérard de Nerval knew what to eat while visiting Brussels, rhapsodising in 1853 about a "a[n] authentic mug of faro, accompanied by one of these....*pistolets* which open in two sandwiches garnished with butter." Belgium's baked goods are often overshadowed by those from its hexagonal neighbour, but de Nerval knew the value of the humble pistolet - a small, round white roll with a little cleft down the middle.

Entrepreneur Valerie Lepla did too, so much so she opened the Pistolet Original *sandwicherie* in Brussels' Sablon neighbourhood in 2013, selling only pistolets - albeit gourmet versions thereof. And like de Nerval, Lepla knew they paired well with Lambic. Faro having disappeared from modern-day Brussels, she stocked her fridge with Brasserie Cantillon's Kriek and Gueuze alongside "Pistolet Original" editions of Brasserie de la Senne's Taras Boulba. Not stopping there, in 2016 she launched a Belgian Hot Dog Pistolet stuffed with sauerkraut cooked in Cantillon Lambic. Lepla then joined forces with chef Dirk Myny of nearby restaurant

Les Brigittines to create with Cantillon an exclusive Geuze called Chouke, made with equal parts one-, two-, and three-year old Lambics aged partly in Armagnac barrels.

Now, Lepla's close cooperation with a local brewery might seem unexceptional. But in 2013, it was still a relative novelty. As any frustrated Belgian beer sommelier knows, the country's chefs have historically treated beer with an indifference bordering on hostility. Some of this is classist, beer being a drink for the café not fine dining. What's more, the country's culinary schools have long placed wine on an unwarranted pedestal, relegating beer to an afterthought.

But there were exceptions. Chefs thoughtful about the beers they served, eager to incorporate beer into their dishes, and eventually becoming evangelists for beer gastronomy. Alain Fayt was an early proselytiser, preaching from his Marollen-based Restobières restaurant since 1987. Olivier Desmet was another, opening Nüetnigenough in a tiny city-centre dining room in 2008. Myny's Les Brigittines championed cooking with, and serving, Lambic, and the restaurant was a regular haunt of Brussels' small coterie of brewers.

Pistolet Original arrived just as the city's culinary establishment was waking up to Brussels' brewing revival. Lepla's (and Desmet's, and Myny's) approach to beer has since, if not quite the rule, become less the exception it used to be. Good, modern beer is no longer unwelcome in Brussels' restaurants, chefs are becoming more involved in the city's beer scene, and the traditional lines separating breweries and restaurants are blurring.

La Fruitiere, for example, has shelves stocked with new wave Brussels beer and developed with Cantillon a Lambic-infused Tomme. Neocantine Liesse, like Pistolet Original, has brewed an in-house beer with Nanobrasserie L'Ermitage. La Tana, a Roman trattoria, excels in serving contemporary Italian, Belgian, and European beer.

Breweries are elbowing in too. In 2019 the Pasta Madre pizzeria opened, a three-way collaboration between Cantillon's Jean Van Roy, Moeder Lambic's Jean Hummler, and Bolognese pizzaïolo Francesco Oppido - with Lambic on the menu, and Lambic (or, at least, Lambic yeast) in the pizzas.

A History of Brussels Beer in 50 Objects

#45
SKOL Bottletop
2010s

- City Life

In 1947, a decade before Léopoldville's Bracongo brewery hired Patrice Lumumba, the Belgian state counted 10 Congolese nationals living in Belgium. Most likely they worked in the office blocks behind the royal palace that housed the network of administrative bodies and industrial concerns comprising Belgium's colonial bureaucracy. Lumumba's period at Bracongo was brief, leaving to lead his country's independence movement, becoming its first Prime Minister before his murder in 1961.

Soon after *Dipenda* Brussels' Congolese population started to grow, as students made their way north to Belgium's universities. Instead of settling near the palace, these new arrivals moved across Brussels' *petite ceinture* to the streets around Porte de Namur, Rue Stassart and the Waversesteenweg. Colloquially dubbed Matongé after Kinshasa's eponymous market district, by the mid-1970s the neighbourhood had evolved into a nightlife district for diplomats, businessmen, students, and politicians - populated by nightclubs and *ngandas* (Lingala for café) serving bottles of Congolese Primus and Skol beer.

The appearance of new drinks and drinking traditions in the wake of new arrivals was nothing new for Brussels. In the mid-19th century, Flemish migrant workers made their homes in the Marollen at the same time as provincial beers from Diest, Leuven and Hoegaarden appeared in estaminets across Brussels. In post-WWII Brussels, it was not Flemish workers but Iberian miners who settled in the streets around Midi station. Portuguese labourers could indulge in Super Bock at the Café 25 Abril on Boulevard Jamar. Their Galician counterparts had the Centro Gallego in nearby St Gilles. For Asturians, there was *Sidra* at Boulevard du Midi's Mar Azul with its murals depicting Asturian mines, or the Centro Cabraliego up on Rue Haute, festooned in Real Oviedo flags. And there was *gambas* and flamenco at El Guadalquivir in the Marollen for their Andalucian compatriots.

Subsequent waves of migration have left a similar mark on Brussels' drinking culture. Central Brussels' Iberian communities were eventually supplanted by a new generation of Maghrébins migration, bringing with it teahouses and shisha bars. The area around the Église Royale Sainte-Marie in Schaarbeek has become synonymous with Brussels' Bulgarian community since its entry into the EU in 2007. Bars serving Kamenitza from Plovdiv or Pirinsko Pivo from Blagoevgrad, with names like Taverna Sofia, share the street with Turkish bakeries selling flatbread and baklava.

Then there's the Portuguese of Flagey, the Romanians around Parc Elisabeth, and the tiny Armenian community in Jette. Even the Irish established a faux-Celtic enclave at Schuman roundabout, where bars like Kitty O'Shea's and the James Joyce supply Brussels' transitory expatriate community with goujons, bacon sandwiches, and Guinness.

Matongé remains, still, important for Brussels' African communities, though its function today is less nightlife district than entry point for people newly arrived from the DRC, Senegal, Guinea and other parts of Central and Equatorial Africa. There are fewer *ngandas* now, and the nightclubs don't have quite the allure they once did. But there's still Skol and Primus in the supermarkets, now joined by a recently - and belatedly - renamed square honouring Congo's most famous beer salesman.

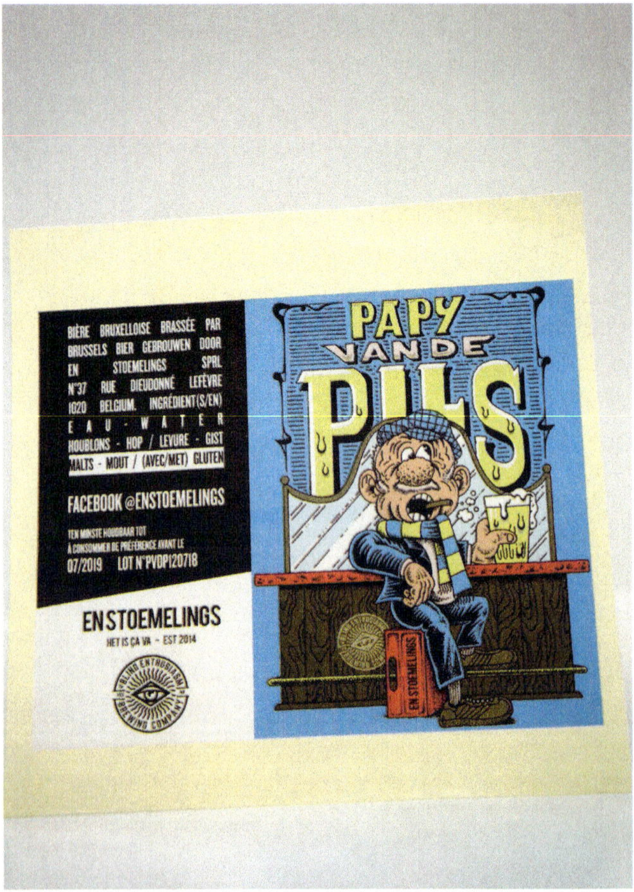
BIÈRE BRUXELLOISE BRASSÉE PAR
BRUSSELS BIER GEBROUWEN DOOR
EN STOEMELINGS SPRL
N°37 RUE DIEUDONNÉ LEFÈVRE
1020 BELGIUM. INGRÉDIENT(S/EN)
EAU - WATER
HOUBLONS - HOP / LEVURE - GIST
MALTS - MOUT / (AVEC/MET) GLUTEN
FACEBOOK @ENSTOEMELINGS
TEN MINSTE HOUDBAAR TOT
À CONSOMMER DE PRÉFÉRENCE AVANT LE
07/2019 LOT N°PVDP120718
ENSTOEMELINGS
HET IS ÇA VA ~ EST 2014
BLIND ENTHUSIASM BREWING COMPANY
PAPY
VAN DE
PILS
EN STOEMELINGS

#46
Papy Van De Pils Label
2018

- Brewery Life

In 2018, a strange fever took hold in Brussels. It was not a new affliction, but when the bacillus responsible last reared its head, it introduced a brewing monoculture that doomed breweries like Leopold, Vandenhuevel, and Roelants to oblivion. Three decades after Wielemans brewed their last bottom-fermented beer, Brussels' brewers had started making Pilsners again.

The first inklings of Pilsner fever's return came in November 2017, when Nanobrasserie L'Ermitage released an exotically-hopped Lager, and followed it up in spring 2018 with a New Zealand-hopped beer for their experimental *Laboratoire d'alchimie* series. These were both one-offs, but more perennial Pilsners were just around the corner. In mid-August 2018, Brasserie En Stoemelings announced they were releasing a new Pilsner - Papy Van De Pils - as a festival exclusive for the forthcoming BXLBeerfest.

Papy was the brewery's first bottom-fermented beer, and their first collaboration (with Blind Enthusiasm Brewing from Edmonton in Canada). It was a light-blond-verging-on-straw beer, bitter, slightly malty, light and refreshing - an *Echte Pils* ("real Pils") according to

En Stoemelings, one which provoked publisher of the now-defunct Belgian Beer and Food Magazine Paul Walsh (no relation) to call it "a...beer that captures everything that's good about beer." A scant two weeks later and Brussels Beer Project were at it, trumpeting a new crowd-sourced core beer called Wunder Lager, a 3.8% hoppy Pale Lager featuring a combination of very un-German Cascade, Citra, Columbus and Mosaic American hop varieties.

Confirmation - if it were needed - that Plisner was becoming endemic in Brussels came the following year, on December 5 2019, when Brasserie de la Senne announced the arrival of Zenne Pils. A German-style Pilsner, its development was aided - thanks to the input of the brewmaster at the Schönram brewery - by Bavarian brewing knowledge, just like its early-20th century predecessors.

It was inevitable that Brussels would succumb to the Pilsner bug. Brussels (and Belgium) has been Pilsner country ever since the style arrived here. The drinkers and brewers alike still consume it in large quantities, making it a lucrative market for the canny breweries able to crack it. There also remains a stubborn nostalgia for the well-made Pilsners of Brussels' post-WWII industrial breweries - witness Brasserie de la Senne name-checking Wiels of Wielemans and Vandenheuvel's Ekla when they launched Zenne Pils.

All it needed for Pilsner to reappear in Brussels was for this new generation of brewers to gain enough confidence at the mash tun to take on the sometimes-unforgiving process of brewing well-made Pilsners. When they did, it wasn't the commodified Pilsner monoculture of their 1950s predecessors that they recreated. Instead, there emerged a diversity of strains, some, like En Stoemelings, de la Senne, and L'Ermitage - who introduced their core range 81 Express Brussels Pilsner in January 2020 - who leaned towards the traditional. And others that exhibited a more pronounced New World influence, represented by Wunder Lager and beers like La Source Beer Co.'s Sour Pils or tropical India Pale Lager.

Either way, after a 30 year interregnum, Brussels was becoming a Pilsner town once again.

A History of Brussels Beer in 50 Objects

#47

L'Ermitage Summer Krump

2019

- Brewery Life

Brussels New Wave

\ ˈbrə-səlz nyü ˈwāv \

Noun

A category of post-2010 new Brussels breweries.

You could call them craft breweries. Or independent breweries. *Bière artisanale* or *ambachtelijk bier*. Whatever you choose, it was clear that by 2020, a new type of Brussels brewery had emerged, taking its place in the canon alongside the city's historical Lambic breweries and its 20th century industrial behemoths.

Brasserie Cantillon had trudged a solo, 20-year furrow as the city's only brewery, inspiring a committed local and international following. But it was Brasserie de la Senne's arrival in December 2010 which launched the Brussels New Wave brewing revival. There was a five-year lag before the number of Brussels breweries doubled again to four, but thereafter the pace picked up. Each subsequent year saw another one or two breweries added to the roster until the number topped out by decade's end at twelve, give or take several edge cases.

These 12 breweries each had their own idiosyncrasies, their own audiences, and each mined their own niche. Distinctive enough, their boosters might say, that corralling them into a single discrete category was a reductive fool's errand. But beyond superficial distinctions, there was a unifying template - albeit one not dissimilar to what English writers Boak and Bailey called the "Global Republic of Craftonia".

A prototypical representative of the Brussels New Wave template was Nanobrasserie L'Ermitage, founded by three men - college friends François Simon, Nacim Menu and Henri Ben Saria. Theirs was a circuitous route into commercial brewing, starting with a shared appreciation for beer before branching into homebrewing, brewing courses, and cuckoo brewing on someone else's equipment. Their Anderlecht brewery, opened in a disused cigarette factory in July 2017, was paid for partially by crowdfunding, and was located in Brussels' canal zone.

None of its founders were graduates of the Cantillon or de la Senne finishing schools, but both breweries had a major influence on L'Ermitage's trajectory. They've collaborated closely with Cantillon and worked with Jean Van Roy on his brewing side-project. De la Senne were, Menu said in a 2018 interview, "like the godfather for [them]", and an inspiration for L'Ermitage's "philosophy…to be brewed in Brussels, and drunk in Brussels."

De la Senne's influence is also there in L'Ermitage's strong visual identity, centred around Alejandro

Jodorowsky-inspired artwork by illustrator Julien Kremer. There are other traits L'Ermitage shares with its Brussels New Wave contemporaries - a flagship Pale Ale (Lanterne), a magpie's eye for beer trends, oenophilia, a willingness to embrace heterodoxy, and comfort in experimenting with mixed fermentation and barrel-ageing.

There is one other characteristic uniting L'Ermitage with its Brussels New Wave contemporaries: on-site drinking. For some, like L'Ermitage, that means a taproom. Others, like Brasserie No Science, have opted for a more ad-hoc, *aperos* approach. Where their 20th century predecessors bequeathed the city towering architectural mastodons, the urban legacy of Brussels' 21st century breweries is likely to be the throwing open of their doors to drinkers and reconfiguring in the process the idea of a modern-day Brussels brewery.

A History of Brussels Beer in 50 Objects

#48

Support Local Breweries T-shirt

2020

- Business Life

Brussels' hospitality industry has a long history of entanglements with public health emergencies. In 1866, 2,732 people died in Brussels' last deadly cholera outbreak (1.5% of the population), with city authorities forced to cancel that autumn's annual festivities. And their contemporary successors have grappled with COVID-19, arriving with a bang on March 12, 2020. That evening, the Belgian government announced the nationwide closure of hospitality businesses, as the country registered its first COVID-19 deaths and case numbers rose exponentially.

The reaction of many in the industry was panic. The livelihoods of bar owners disappeared, and breweries overwhelmingly reliant on horeca - some for up to 95% of their sales - saw their primary income stream vanish. But there was resolve, too, as business owners made drastic, often unexpected, decisions to survive. Breweries halted production, and within a week, several had launched webshops. Soon, bike couriers criss-crossed Brussels, cargo bikes laden down with beer from En Stoemelings, L'Ermitage or de la Senne.

Bars like Dynamo in St Gilles and Dekkera did likewise, liquidating excess stock to stay afloat.

As it became clear neither COVID nor public health restrictions were going anywhere, more improbable things occurred - like a national supermarket stocking Taras Boulba, a necessary reversal of Brasserie de la Senne's long-stated policy of only supplying local and independent shops.

Where there was resolve, there was also solidarity. Larger breweries stocked the beers of smaller colleagues on their webshops. En Stoemelings used their lockdown beer delivery service to raise money for local charities, raising €5,000 by early April 2020. Together with Brussels Beer Project, La Source Beer Co., and No Science, they also repurposed 1,000 litres of unused beer into an Iris flower-infused spirit with the help of a local distillery.

The privations visited on Brussels by the pandemic also undermined, briefly, long-standing factional differences in the city's beer community. In May 2020 a nine-strong brewery collective released a limited-edition "Support your local brewer" t-shirt, printed with the name of each brewery (including Brussels Beer Project and Brasserie de la Senne), with a portion of the sales going to a hospitality support fund.

Restrictions for the hospitality industry waxed and waned alongside fluctuating infection rates until spring 2022, when the last of them were finally removed. Some bars never reopened, others did so under new management or pivoted to new concepts. The focus for now is on survival, and working off the debt accrued during the lockdown years.

In the wake of 1866's cholera outbreak, Brussels' politicians decided to bury the source of the outbreak - a foetid Zenne river - underground. The massive public works that followed demolished parts of central Brussels and virtually all the breweries located therein, reshaping forever the city's brewing history. It looks as if, for now, today's brewers and bar owners have avoided a similarly catastrophic fate. It's too early to tell yet what the long-term impact of the pandemic will be, but whatever they are, we will likely be living with them for some time to come.

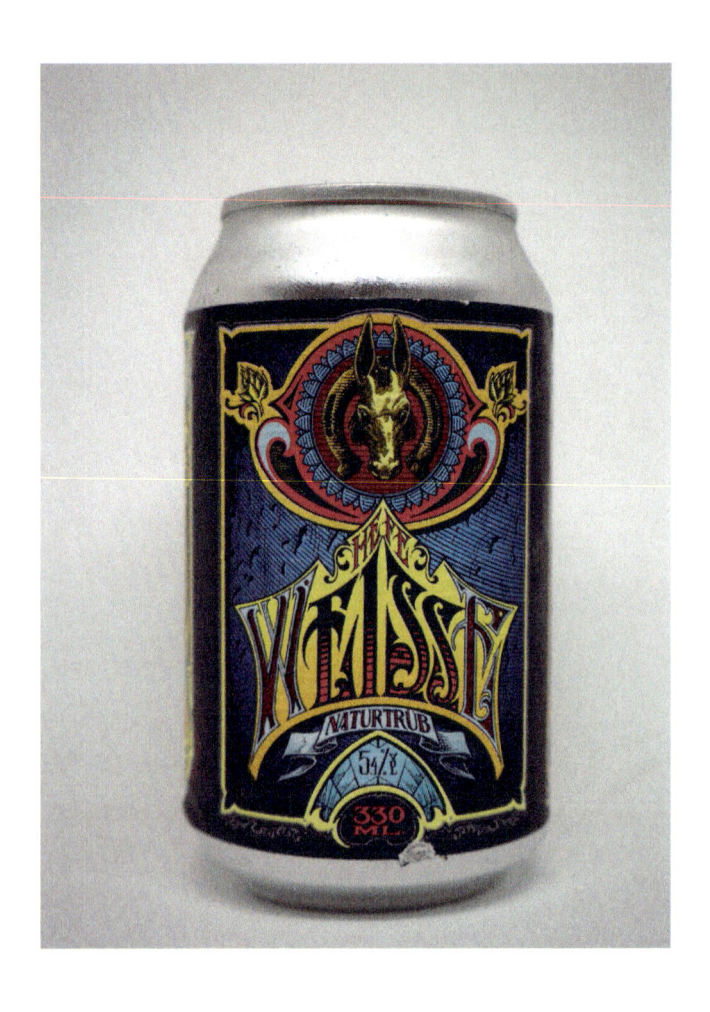

A History of Brussels Beer in 50 Objects

#49

Brasserie de la Mule Hefe Weisse

2021

- Brewery Life

"It is not worthwhile to try to keep history from repeating itself, for man's character will always make the preventing of the repetitions impossible." - Mark Twain

Once upon a time in Brussels, Bavarian bottom-fermented beers vied with English Pale Ales and Porters for supremacy. Brewed on German equipment by German brewmasters, Bocks and Bavières dominated brewing from the 1860s until 1914, after which local breweries switched their allegiances to homegrown Stouts and Scotch Ales.

Neither trend survived the 20th century. Grande Brasserie de Koekelberg, the last of Brussels' German-inspired industrial breweries, closed in the late-1960s. 20 years later Wielemans-Ceuppens, loyal proponents of the English tendency, followed them into oblivion. But, as Samuel Clemens' alter ego said, there's nothing new under the sun - and certainly not in brewing.

And so, as the Brussels New Wave beer movement bounded into its second decade, history began repeating itself, in reverse chronological order. First came

Brasserie La Jungle in early 2021 with the launch of an English Golden Ale. Brewing in an abandoned textile factory in Anderlecht, La Jungle firmly nailed their colours to the English mast by following up with an English Porter and English Bitter brewed with Kentish hops.

Brasserie de la Mule was next, looking east rather than across the Channel. Ex-Brasserie de la Senne brewer Joël Galy opened Mule in April 2021 in Schaarbeek, naming it after the neighbourhood's mascots, the donkeys who transported Schaarbeekse Krieken from nearby orchards into Brussels for use in Kriekenlambiek. But despite also having done time with Brasserie Cantillon, Galy didn't choose something spontaneously-fermented as Mule's first beer. Instead, he brewed in the Bavarian tradition - a Hefe Weisse Naturtrüb wheat beer, which was soon followed by a Lager, Helles, Berliner Weisse, Kölsch, Dunkel Weisse, and even an homage to one of his favourite beers, Schneider Weisse's Mein Hopfenweisse.

It's unlikely either breweries took direct inspiration from their predecessors, and alongside these foreign styles they also produce more recognisably Belgian beers - Saisons, Blondes, Grisettes, and Table Beer. But in seeking a point of distinction in an increasingly (relatively) crowded market place they are not so much different from 19th century brewers betting on Bavarian beers, or their 1920s successors emulating their English counterparts.

Instead, these decisions are reflective of a maturing

beer scene. There's a new generation of brewers more confident in their abilities and their taste in beer. Sufficiently acclimatised to the world of Sours, IPAs, and Imperial Stouts, local drinkers are more adventurous too, and now there's a whole ecosystem willing to encourage brewers in their gambles. It would have been unfathomable even a few years ago to think somewhere like Gist could put on an evening of La Jungle cask ales and sell out in hours. But they did. Repeatedly.

What the trajectories of La Jungle and Mule suggest is that Brussels beer is heading in unexpected - if occasionally familiar - directions. All we need now is for someone to convince Galy to brew a Bock beer and the circle really will be complete.

A History of Brussels Beer in 50 Objects

#50

Brussels Beer Project Coolship

2021

- Brewery Life

So the last shall be first, and the first last.

This series started with a coolship, so it feels appropriate to finish with one. In December 2021, Brussels Beer Project publicly announced what was both the worst kept secret and the most unexpected recent development in Brussels beer: they had started brewing Lambic. They did so in a quintessentially Brussels Beer Project manner - by wheeling one of their coolships onto the Grand Place and parking within a couple of metres of the *Brouwershuis*, the centuries-long seat of brewing power in Brussels.

This would all have sounded preposterous to a Brussels beer drinker in 2012 still acclimatising to the city having not one but *two* local breweries. But a lot can change in ten years, and within a decade of Brasserie de la Senne's arrival in 2010, the city's new brewers were confident enough in their *métier* to take on the city's native brewing tradition.

With the arrival of a second Lambic brewery (and with a *third* one announced since BBP's stunt), it increasingly feels in 2022 as if many generations of Brussels' beer history have collapsed in on themselves, and we're experiencing all of them concurrently. There are the IPAs and Americana of the Brussels New Wave. Breweries like En Stoemelings and de la Senne keep the flame lit for Belgium's ecclesiastic and agricultural traditions. Local Pilsners share shelf space next to English Ales and Reinheitsgebot-compliant Lagers.

The neighbourhoods along the Brussels-Charleroi canal are once again fragrant with brewing activity, as new breweries emerge within sight of the relics of the city's 20th century brewery construction boom. Breweries have also returned to central Brussels and to the industry's spiritual and historical home in the streets around Place St Géry; there are even rumours of Lambic barrels maturing in the market hall's vaulted cellars.

Nearby, the grave of the city's mythical beer king Gambrinus is being prepared for a new home in the under-construction Belgian Beer World experience occupying the Bourse. With the return of post-pandemic uncertainty and plans to disinter the Zenne river from its concrete sarcophagus below the streets of Brussels, all that's left is for some enterprising brewer to rediscover a medieval *Waeghbaert* recipe and every facet of Brussels' long beer history would be represented.

Alongside these stories and their totemic objects are other stories for which there was not enough space. The role, for example, of women. Or how the Zenne river influenced, and was influenced by, the city's breweries. Or the Italo-Belgian mutual appreciation society expressed in every plate of brasserie *spaghetti bolognaise* and in every bottle of Cantillon grape Lambic.

But space was limited and my choices were subjective. Even so, these 50 objects tell a story. One about the intertwined histories of a city and its breweries. About what they brewed and why they brewed. About dusky cafés and dead-end *estaminets*. And about all the Brusselaars - the *Zagenmannekens* and the *Pottezuipers*, the exiles and the new arrivals - who've ever enjoyed a glass of Lambic.

Selected bibliography

More information on the sources used in the writing of this book can be found at the Brussels Beer City website, on the individual object articles: www.beercity.brussels/history-brussels-beer-50-objects.

Below is a collection of books, magazines, articles, and useful online sources without which this book would not have been possible.

Books and Magazines

Around Brussels in 80 Beers, Joe Stange and Yvan De Baets, 2009: Cogan and Mater

Bier et Brouwerijen te Brussel, Patricia Quintens, 1996: AMVB

Brussels: A cultural and literary history, André De Vries, Signal Books, 2002

Cahier 8: Bières, brasseries, patrimoine industriel, La Fonderie, 1990

Congo 1885-1960: Een financieel-economische geschiedenis, Frans Beulens, 2007: EPO

Congo. Een geschiedenis, David Van Reybrouck, 2007: De Bezije Bij

Constant vanden Stock: Een leven, twee carriers, Hugo Camps, Kritak/Thomas Rap, 1993

De Brouwerij van Ghlin, Brasserie du Ghlin, 1962

De Buik van Brussel, Lucas Catherine, 2019: EPO

De cafés van Brussel, in de reeks: Brussel, stad van kunst en geschiedenis, Anne-Marie Pirlot, 2004: Monumenten en Landschappen

Dictionnaire du dialecte bruxellois, Louis Quievreux, 2015: Regionalismes

Estaminets et cafés : Histoires bruxelloises, Thérèse Symons, Sylvie Lefebvre and Yannik van Praag, 2018: BruxellesFabriques

Expo 58 en zijn bierbrouwers, François Van Kerckhoven, boekscout.nl, 2013.

Ganshoren tussen stad en natuur, Géry Leloutre and Hubert Lionnez, 2013: Erfgoedcel Brussel

Geuze & Kriek, Jef Vanden Steen, Lannoo, 2011

Geuze en Humanisme: zelfgenoegzame beschouwingen over de voortreffelijkheid van het bier van Brussel en Brabant en van de mensen die het drinken, Hubert van Herreweghen, P Uitgeverij, 1955

Gruuten Dëst. 101 Toffe cafés & kroegen in Brussel en omgeving, Sven Gatz, Marc Gatz, and Karel Adriansens 2002: Oogachtend

Het voormalige Coudenbergpaleis, Pierre Anagnostopoulos and Jean Houssiau, 2010: Erfgoedcel Brussel

Koekelberg Au fil du temps... Au coeur des rues..., Didier Sutter, Drukker, 2012

La fabrication moderne de la bière, Brasserie Vandenheuvel, 1955

Le Mariage de Mlle Beulemans, Frantz Fonson and Fernand Wicheler, 1910 (2015): Espace Nord

Les mémoires de Jef Lambic, Robert Dessart, La technique belge: 1955

Midi Del Sur, Jeroen De Smet en Hans Vandecandelaere, 2010: Erfgoedcel Brussel

Tome II - Les vieux estaminets de Bruxelles et environs, Robert Desart & Marinus, Albert (préface)

W: Zeven wandelingen rondom Wielemans-Ceuppens, Zimmerfrei, Wiels, 2013

Websites

Archives de Bruxelles: https://archives.bruxelles.be/

BelgicaPress: https://www.belgicapress.be/index.php

Bruciel: https://bruciel.brussels/

Bruzz: https://www.bruzz.be/

C'était au temps où Bruxelles brassait (Guy Moerenhout): https://biereetbrasseriesbruxelles.wordpress.com/

Centrum Agrarische Geschiedenis (Cagnet): https://www.belgicapress.be/index.php

Lambic.info: http://www.lambic.info/Home

Lost Beers: https://lostbeers.com

Reflexcity: https://www.reflexcity.net/

Wielemans Machines: https://wielemansmachines.wixsite.com/english/history

"A History of Brussels Beer in 50 Objects" audioguide walking tour

To accompany the publication of this book, an interactive audioguide/walking tour has been produced - allowing readers and listeners to experience the stories told and the objects included here.

Scan the code below (or visit beercity.brussels/50-objects-walking-tour) and rediscover the world of Brussels beer history in the places where it happened

Acknowledgements

"A History of Brussels Beer In 50 Objects" would not have been possible without the cooperation and support of the following people and institutions, to whom I am hugely indebted: Thierry Van Linthoudt for his extensive collection of beer history, Jean Van Roy, Marieke De Baerdemaeker at the Museum van de Stad Brussel, Savinien Peeters of La Fonderie, Luís Bekaert of Lovulum, Antoine Pierson of Malt Attacks, Jean Goovaerts, Annelies Tollet, the Centrum Agrarische Geschiedenis, and the illustrators and breweries that have given their permission for their work to be reproduced.

The same goes for everyone who has encouraged me in this project, including Boak and Bailey, Joe Stange, Sven Gatz, Breandán Kearney, and Jeff Alworth.

Huge thanks to Ruairí for the typsetting, and to Louise for the cover design.

About the Author

Award-winning beer writer Eoghan Walsh founded the website Brussels Beer City in 2017.

His work has featured in Belgian Beer and Food, Good Beer Hunting, Pellicle, and The Irish Times. Eoghan has won numerous awards, including Best Young Beer Writer of the Year 2018, five gold medals from the North American Guild of Beer Writers, and has been shortlisted for the Beer Writing Award at The Irish Food Writing Awards.